Twentieth - Century
Embroidery
in Great Britain 1964~1977

Constance Howard

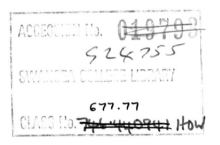
B T BATSFORD LTD   LONDON

Acknowledgment

So many people have given me help and advice that it is difficult to know where to begin. First of all I would like to thank everyone who has kindly contributed photographs or information or both to the book; as well as answering numerous queries.

Especially I would like to thank my daughter for her tolerance in deciphering my writing and in improving my English as well as correcting sundry other faults in the manuscript while typing the book; also Thelma M. Nye for being so patient in waiting for its final chapter, and the Embroiderers' Guild for their very generous help in finding appropriate works to be photographed and the time involved in doing this research.

Finally I would like to thank Nick Nicholson of Hawkley Studios for his excellent photographs which enhance the appearance of the book.

Chiswick 1985   CH

The text covers fourteen years of embroidery during which time some of the most important developments have taken place.

Embroiderers not mentioned specifically in this text will be included in the next volume together with all the biographies.

ISBN 0 713 4227 1

Filmset in Monophoto Times New Roman by Servis Filmsetting Ltd, Manchester and printed in Great Britain by Butler & Tanner Ltd, Frome, Somerset for the publishers B T Batsford Ltd 4 Fitzhardinge Street London W1H 0AH

Contents

Introduction

The gradual change in attitudes to embroidery was noticeable in the late fifties, since when education and the reorganisation of public examinations in art and crafts, with design of major consideration, has had an enormous effect on embroidery throughout England. Television programmes on art and crafts have been shown to a diverse audience and have helped to spread knowledge and appreciation of the crafts and their content as art forms. Exhibitions in museums and galleries over the last 20 years have shown the public a variety of approaches to embroidery from the design and technical viewpoints; the end of year shows in colleges of art, polytechnics, colleges of education and other educational establishments have demonstrated the raising of standards of embroidery over the years, from a craft to a subject with a strong art content.

The manufacture of new materials, wider use of machine embroidery and the greater freedom of students to pursue their own inclinations, have led to more experiment and enterprise. Innovative ideas have developed from mixed media, both successful and less successful, but necessary if an art is to grow and stay alive. Crazes have come and gone, from Berlin woolwork, art needlework, the penchant for ecclesiastical banners, embroidery on dress and patchwork, to return again in slightly different guises. Styles in design have waxed and waned, from the copying of paintings for canvas work, geometric pattern, abstraction, illustration, back to realism, and to the use of newspaper photographs as design sources. The decoration of household articles has been in and out of fashion but the wall hanging or panel as a vehicle for embroidery has continued up to the present as a favourite article for embellishment. Ecclesiastical embroidery during the last 20 years has been given impetus by the Church, with commissions for both old and new establishments.

When asked 'Where do you think embroidery is going?', I do not know the answer. There is a tendency today to use wood, metal, plaster and other non-textile materials, rather than to exploit the use of threads and fabrics and to demonstrate what can be done with them. It is necessary to experiment, and the younger student should, if anything, be extreme in outlook, provided that the foundation training is sound enough to be at times forgotten. New ideas are always required and any art or craft that becomes stereotyped loses its vitality, eventually dying, but to ignore the superb qualities of threads and fabrics, with their endless possibilities for design and stitchery, does seem a pity.

1 1970 – Margaret Meliar-Smith. *Cows in a Copse.* A panel 18½ in. (47 cm) square. Machine embroidery on a pale orange background. The leaves are applied in dark grey and orange shot fabric. Grey, pale turquoise, orange, pink and cyclamen coloured threads; the cows are stitched with machine whipping and straight stitching in grey thread. *Photograph by Hawkley Studios*

The Sixties

At the end of 1963, just before embroidery was introduced as a subject in the new examinations, exhibitions continued to be a source of ideas to both embroiderers and the public. These exhibitions stimulated wider public interest and encouraged the clergy to give more commissions for the Church. The greater availability of materials and threads was also an incentive. Enterprise by young dress designers, some of whom used embroidery in their creations, and a general increase of vitality in work produced by students, encouraged the embroiderer to strive towards better standards. These factors each contributed to the recognition of embroidery as both an art and a craft.

Art examinations **The National Diploma in Art and Design (NDAD)**

With the introduction of the new art examinations in 1963 conducted by the Council for Academic Awards, the greater freedom given to selected colleges to make their own programmes resulted in a considerable development in textile arts. Embroidery was included as a subject in 1964, now becoming a part of the textile/fashion area of design.

In 1964 Goldsmiths' School of Art, as a place of a suitable standard, was allowed to take students for the examinations, with embroidery as the main subject and printed textiles and weaving as supporting subjects. For this examination a syllabus based on a general art background was planned, all courses aiming to keep a high level of achievement. Before students were interviewed for acceptance on a course, they would previously have taken a year, and sometimes two years, of foundation work. Acceptance meant three more years of study, at the end of which a diploma was given to a student who had reached the necessary standard. This standard rose considerably during the ensuing years and embroidery developed further with ideas becoming livelier and more individual. Birmingham, Loughborough and Manchester Colleges of Art were selected as diploma centres during the next few years. **Joan Cleaver** was in charge of embroidery in Birmingham, **Alison Liley** for a few years at Loughborough, while **Lilla Speir** was at Manchester College of Art.

A stipulation of this new diploma course was that full-time students only could be accepted. Each college devised its own syllabus; continuous internal assessments were given with an external assessment in the final year. The qualification in whatever specialisation the student worked led to the National Diploma in Art and Design (NDAD).

A more experimental attitude to embroidery was introduced with this new Diploma, each student being encouraged to find her own way of working and expressing ideas. A broader approach to the subject and other areas of art were fostered by the lectures on the history of art and design, now a compulsory part of the courses for all students. These lectures gave a background against which embroidery could be put into its historic context in relation to other arts and crafts, giving at the same time a wider view of their interdependence. Many students who had studied the history of embroidery previously, had not related it to other contemporary forms of art such as painting and sculpture or crafts such as metalwork and jewellery. Matisse with his strong sense of colour and design, Paul Klee with his feeling for pattern, Van Gogh with his textured surfaces and Chagall with his compositions of space and movement were just names to many textile students, but with this general art history the work of these artists and others generated meaning and an awareness of factors which led to a more analytical appraisal on the part of the students and what they were attempting to do.

The Diploma in Scotland

In Scotland, the art schools in Aberdeen, Dundee, Edinburgh and Glasgow, where embroidery was a main subject, gave a Diploma in Art (DA) until 1978. **Crissie White**, Head of the Department of Embroidered and Woven Textiles, at Glasgow School of Art, and **Kathleen Whyte**, together with the Academic Registrar of Glasgow School of Art, have supplied the following information on education in art in these Scottish schools of art.

The educational system in the four schools was different from that in England, being a four-year course at the end of which a Diploma in Art and Design was awarded. This system commenced in 1920, allowing the staff in the schools to organise their own courses. The Needlework Development Scheme, too, started in Scotland in 1934, but became available in England after the Second World War.

Common external assessors visited the four schools in turn, submitting reports both to the schools and to the Scottish Education Department. By this means an overall high standard of work and course development was maintained.

Kathleen Whyte, the previous Head of Embroidered and Woven Textiles, was a member of the team involved by the Department of Education and Science in approving courses within the colleges of art in England, when the original Diploma in Art and Design was awarded. This was transferred to the Council for National Academic Awards, later becoming a BA honours degree in art. In 1975 the Glasgow School of Art applied for approval of an honours degree in fine art and design, which was granted in 1976. Duncan of Jordanstone College of Art, Dundee, Grays School of Art, Aberdeen, part of Robert Gordon's Technical College, all followed, with courses now approved. Edinburgh College of Art in conjunction with Heriot Watt University also offer degrees. These qualifications, whether degrees or diplomas, have been the background for all Scottish teachers of art. In Scotland the practice of providing teachers of art from colleges of education was never introduced. The attitude to the training of Scottish art teachers has been that they should in the first instance be professional artists. Glasgow School of Art is now the only Scottish school where embroidery is a degree course. In Dundee it may be studied as a second subject. Degrees in other colleges are not in embroidery.

Education Embroidery in schools and colleges

Embroidery in schools is a subject for the CSE examinations and for O and A levels. As I was an examiner for 11 years for O and A levels embroidery, I had some insight into the standards of both written and practical papers. Very few schools were able to maintain both written and practical work to an equally high standard; the secondary modern schools and some of the comprehensive schools produced individual embroidery using fabrics and threads imaginatively, but written work was obviously of less interest and importance and these same children were rarely able to express on paper what they knew or understood. Conversely, those children in grammar schools and others of a similar nature wrote well or adequately on history and methods but their practical work, I found, was often dull and lacking in spontaneity or life. The schools where both O and A levels papers in embroidery were well carried out showed that the instruction was balanced but the teachers allowed the children to experiment and to make personal choices of materials, while interest in methods and in history had been stimulated by teachers who were themselves keen on linking theory and practice.

In some of the comprehensive schools both boys and girls were producing embroidery of merit. **Joan Thewsey** at Tollington Park Comprehensive School in London said that much had been done during the past few years to encourage the development of the craft as a vital, creative means of expression. This had been fostered by shows of work in colleges and schools of art and by group exhibitions of professional embroiderers. She said 'it is possible to create in stitch and appliqué, forms with intensity of feeling and individual vitality, as valid and inescapable as personal statements in painting, collage and sculpture . . . it is difficult to define sculptured painting, a stitch collage, an embroidered sculpture . . . If truly creative embroidery is to be achieved . . . personal experience has to be built up by a carefully planned diet of design and colour research, practical experiment and study . . . of historical and contemporary works'. (*Embroidery*, Volume XXI, Number 1, Spring 1970.)

In the training colleges where needlework was taught as an art and a craft, with embroidery of more importance than making garments, students appreciated the aesthetics of the craft so were able to instil this approach in schools when the opportunity arose. Those students on domestic science courses often approached embroidery from the technical angle and from its use in the home, with little design or colour instruction, but as the decade advanced more colleges were aware of the importance of art in the domestic science departments and specialists were employed to teach art and colour related to the home. This had a beneficial effect on those students now on such courses, and consequently on their teaching when they obtained posts in schools. Where the art teacher and domestic science or needlework teachers collaborated, embroidery became a lively part of the curriculum, as it did where the art and craft teacher was one person, or the art teacher and the craft teacher worked together. The CSE examination allowed more freedom for the child to experiment and to produce individual work for assessment thus giving the opportunity for initiative.

Ravensbourne College film

At the end of the 1960s an enterprising project 'The Growing Art of Embroidery' was carried out by the television and film department of the Ravensbourne College of Art. This was the inspiration of Miss **N L Tracey**, Head of the dress and embroidery department at Stockwell College of Education, Bromley, who produced the film with some members of her department. The reasons for making the film were 'to show the development of a creative craft through school learning; to enable schools to use the film for study and as stills for teaching aids and to show the uses of embroideries such as wall hangings and ecclesiastical vestments in a contemporary way', (*Embroidery*, Volume XX, Number 2, Summer 1969.)

Gawthorpe Hall

A scheme that was to become a reality was the recognition of Gawthorpe Hall as a study centre. An appeal in 1965 by **C Maisie Currey** in the Summer number of *Embroidery* was for an awareness of the fact that Gawthorpe Hall could become a centre for craft education if money was forthcoming for the maintenance of the building, and also for the collection. The Hall, already open for visits and for private study, could no longer be maintained without care, neither could the collection. **Rachel Kay Shuttleworth** and her committee and the Gawthorpe Foundation hoped that the Hall could become a centre for the study of textiles and during the summer of 1965 only, an education programme of day lectures, concerts and drama was given. The collection, already well known, was visited by teachers and students, by textile designers and those in industry.

In 1967 Rachel Kay Shuttleworth died, leaving her magnificent collection of costume, embroidery, lace, accessories and books for study by students and others at Gawthorpe Hall. After her death the Hall was offered for lease and was accepted by Lancashire Education Authority in 1970 as a study centre for textiles, for courses and lectures. It was under the administration of Nelson and Colne College with a member of staff appointed as a part-time curator of the textiles and a part-time lecturer in the College. Exhibitions of work from the collection are now arranged as well as those by artists invited, from time to time, to show their work in the exhibition gallery.

Victoria and Albert Museum lectures

Joan Edwards, who studied embroidery during the fifties, wrote *Bead Embroidery* for Batsford in 1966 and also became a panel lecturer for embroidery at the Victoria and Albert Museum, in the Education Department. **Madeleine Mainstone**, Keeper of the Department, instituted the course in order to acquaint embroiderers with the resources of the Museum and to show how they could be used to their fullest extent.

This series of lectures by Joan Edwards became known aś the 'ten-week course in embroidery'. Each week a different aspect of the craft was studied, an aim being to follow techniques and their development throughout the centuries and to relate embroidery to different collections in the Museum. It was emphasised that embroidery showed similar design characteristics to other decorative arts of the same period.

The Royal School of Needlework certificate course

The Royal School of Needlework during the sixties and seventies continued the two-year certificate course for apprentices, some of those trained becoming members of the workroom staff with, in the third year, an opportunity to take the City and Guilds of London Institute examinations in embroidery.

Conservation of embroidery and tapestry was also undertaken, and private commissions carried out, often designed by non-members of the Royal School of Needlework. The *Hastings Tapestry*, commissioned in 1960, was designed and carried out in the workroom (see page 19); the *Overlord* embroidery was designed by Sandra Lawrence having been commissioned by Lord Dulverton in 1969 and taking five years to complete (see page 88).

Exhibitions

As a source of ideas and education in crafts, embroidery selected by professional artists for public exhibition was generally stimulating. In the early sixties, at Interiors International, **Jennifer Gray**, **Alison Liley** (née Erridge) and **Joy Clucas** (née Dobbs) showed panels mainly machine embroidered which were arranged within room settings (colour plate 3). Other shows opened people's eyes to the changes that were taking place in the crafts, embroidery being a prominent part of a series of exhibitions called 'Contemporary Hangings', the first of which was held in 1965.

'Contemporary Hangings' exhibition

Vera Sherman trained as a painter, later studied sculpture and became an art correspondent for the Italian magazine *D'Ars*. Through this work she realised that the general public had little opportunity to learn about the artist-craftsman in the field of embroidery and textiles. She found gallery directors unwilling to give space to these forms of art and had previously discussed this attitude with John Eveleigh, the Director of the New Metropole Arts Centre in Folkestone. In 1964 Barnett Field, an enthusiast in the biannual International Folklore Festival held in Folkestone, asked the Director if Vera Sherman could put on an exhibition suited to the Festival. Having talked about this possibility before, in June 1965 she was able to arrange a show of textiles at the Arts Centre, including batik, embroidery, fabric collage and tapestry. This exhibition created a great deal of interest and was the first of a number of shows of Contemporary Hangings to tour the country. It is worth quoting a part of Vera Sherman's introduction to the catalogue which is a précis of the history of wall hangings and concludes with today's artist-craftsman. She says: 'The artist-craftsman of today has a great heritage to which he owes much, but he is of today, and this is an exciting time for him. He has new concepts of contemporary design to explore, new materials are at his disposal, there are new technical advances in industry which he can adapt to his own requirements. Nevertheless his task is not an easy one. The medium he has chosen is time absorbing. . . . In this mechanical age, when time is at such a premium, the revived interest in the work of the artist-craftsman is encouraging'. Among those embroiderers invited to participate in the first show were Joy Clucas, Rosalind Floyd and Margaret Kaye while Vera Sherman showed collage. See figure 14.

A second showing of 'Contemporary Hangings' took place in London in October 1966. This was collected and organised by Vera Sherman again and contained work by embroiderers, weavers and others who created and decorated fabrics, using dyes, threads and collage. Three embroiderers new to the exhibition were **Anne Butler**, **Janet Graham** and **Eirian Short**, all from Goldsmiths' School of Art. This exhibition and the smaller 'Contemporary Pictures in Fabric and Thread' were both promoted by Vera Sherman and travelled round the country, as did exhibitions assembled by the '62 Group. These all contributed a valuable insight into what was current in embroidery and allied textile crafts and were of particular interest to those people in areas where exhibitions of textiles were rare.

The exhibitions of Contemporary Hangings continued for ten years, with seven travelling shows, while there were three collections of Contemporary Pictures in Fabric and Thread as well as special collections, all on tour.

ILEA exhibition

Another exhibition that showed the increasing interest by schools practising embroidery, was arranged in 1966, where work selected by the Inner London Education Authority was displayed at the South London Art Gallery. It was to demonstrate the potential of embroidery as education. Work from a wide range of age groups was shown, from infant level to examples from schools and colleges of art in the London area, illustrating the advancement of the craft since the Second World War.

Embroidery as an Education – conference

A conference entitled 'Embroidery as an Education' took place in September 1969, with Dorothy Allsopp as chairman. Iris Hills, Margaret Nicholson and I were among the speakers. (In September 1966, Iris Hills had joined Dorothy Allsopp as an inspector of further and higher education with the Inner London Education Authority.) Joan Edwards talked on museum services and Lynette de Denne on the Embroiderers' Guild in education. Various points were discussed such as guidance in using museums, the value of critical appraisal and the encouragement of a variety of types of work which the conference felt was important.

Embroiderers' Guild

Children's classes

In 1963 a venture by the Embroiderers' Guild during mornings of the school holidays was conducted by Lynette de Denne. Both boys and girls from seven to 15 years of age attended classes for embroidery.

Challenge Cup competitions

The Embroiderers' Guild Challenge Cup competitions continued. Ecclesiastical embroidery was awarded the Members' Cup in 1963. Machine embroidery was a feature of wall decorations, while some examples showed a combination of hand and machine embroidery. The affiliated groups entered ecclesiastical and household articles. In the schools section the same year, work of individual merit, without strong evidence of influence by the teacher, was praised. Although there was good work, some of it reflected earlier examples, lack of individuality was evident in others and, according to the review, standards were mixed. The Mary Boon Secondary School for Girls won the Senior Schools Challenge Cup, as it had done previously, and in 1966 won the Advanced Senior Schools Challenge Cup, winning it again in 1967. (*Embroidery*, Volume XIX, Spring 1968.)

The Members' Challenge Cup competition was separated into two parts in 1967, one for those without a qualification and another for those with a qualification. In 1968 the competition showed a better standard of work as well as an increase in the number of entries which, during previous years, had been falling off. The group showing qualified members' work contained mainly panels while the work of unqualified members showed an opposite tendency with one third panels, the rest articles with a particular purpose, among which was ecclesiastical embroidery. (*Embroidery*, Volume XIX, Number 3, Autumn 1968.)

A new venture by the Guild was the inauguration in June 1969 of summer holiday competitions for children. By these it was hoped to encourage an interest in embroidery. The age limits were under 18, under 12, and under seven years of age. Photographs were printed in *Embroidery* magazine, from which the competitors were to make their own interpretations in fabric, threads and beads. A number of children rose to the challenge, Bridget Pavitt one of them. See figure 52.

Embroiderers' Guild Diamond Jubilee

The oustanding event of the decade for the Guild was in 1966 which marked its Diamond Jubilee. A special issue of *Embroidery* was published, containing articles on different aspects of the craft written by well-known embroiderers. **Kathleen Whyte** on 'Thinking Towards Design' said 'we are concerned . . . to foster individuality . . . the embroiderer must be both designer and craftsman'. She suggested that today might be known as 'the Period of Collage'. . . . 'The relationship of threads to materials is the essence of embroidery. Threads create infinitely varied qualities of line, ranging in comparable scale from fine sensitive pen line to bold free brush stroke.' Further that 'there is nothing hidebound about the words stitchery and techniques – stitches are ways of invention by which we create new techniques'. She also said that 'the danger of working directly on fabric could result in a lack of structure, on the other hand the idea could become dead if too complete on paper'.

Beryl Dean stressed again the need for better design and an openminded outlook by the clergy, which was necessary if ecclesiastical embroidery was to advance to the standard of some of the European work. She mentioned embroidery in exhibitions and the disappointment of those who had entered work that was rejected, this usually due to very poor design, unsuitability for its purpose or for other valid reasons. An analysis of how she planned and worked out a commissioned design for embroidery for a church, with the trials and errors involved in the initial stages, was a part of her article and her final words were 'church embroidery combining hand and machine is really alive today'.

My plea was that good embroidery was often produced by an artist-craftsman of a standard comparable to that of a highly regarded 'fine' artist who was both a painter and a mural decorator. Works by both artists, having a purpose, could be termed 'applied art' and if the level of attainment of each was equally high they should be recognised as of equal standing as artists. The article was a plea that embroidery at its best should be recognised as an art as serious and intellectual in content as 'fine art'.

Pat Russell explained that letters were 'abstract forms' and if regarded as Chinese or Greek characters, which most of us do not read but look at as patterns, they could be simpler to use and produce better results. She also said that lettering must be incorporated at the beginning of a design if to be used.

Dorothy Allsopp wrote on the value of embroidery in further education and the satisfaction derived by students in 'practising a creative craft' or in working with others. She also discussed the part that the tutor played in adult education and the need to know when to 'deal sympathetically with early struggles . . . when to press for greater achievement without discouraging the student'. Her final words were that 'All experiences which come through the broad study and practice of this craft add up to the enrichment and fulfilment of life which is surely the aim of all further education'.

A design for a transfer to mark the occasion of the Diamond Jubilee was drawn by **Margaret Nicholson**. This was a small panel of the figure of St Clare of Assisi, the patron saint of embroiderers. Eight volunteers offered to work the saint in their own ways for this Jubilee celebration. Figures 25, 26 and 27 show some of these ideas.

The Diamond Jubilee exhibition at the Commonwealth institute attracted many people who found a high standard of work both in design and technique, particularly as much of it was by non-professional embroiderers. Wall hangings, mainly abstract in style, formed the majority of exhibits. Several artists wrote comments on the exhibition in the Autumn number of *Embroidery* (Volume 17, No. 3, 1966). **Dorothy Darch** maintained that 'all true art must be a reflection of its own time . . . and as an artist expresses his thoughts and emotions through painting so the personality of the designer must project through the embroidery. In this way embroidery is just as much an art as painting'. She also stressed the importance of experiment and that embroidery was no longer a feminine craft.

Joy Clucas said that a more expressive interpretation of embroidery was taking place and hoped that 'there will emerge trends of finer drawing, greater individuality . . . and an absence of gimmickry'. She wondered whether the additions of extraneous objects were gimmicks and mentioned the sewing machine as 'the fabric artist's more versatile tool'. Other artists contributed comments; also artists mentioned already in *Twentieth-Century Embroidery 1940–1963*, showed work, among these Jennifer Gray and Isabel Clover (49) who received an award for an embroidered 'Chess Box'. Beryl Dean showed a dossal in the exhibition.

Appeal fund

An appeal fund for the Embroiderers' Guild Headquarters was launched in the summer of 1967, with an exhibition of work carried out in the classes that were part of the Guild's regular programme for afternoon and evening sessions.

The '62 Group

The '62 Group continued to hold exhibitions and its fourth travelling show was arranged in April 1964, so reaching different parts of the country. In July another '62 Group exhibition showed mainly collage which shocked some people with its non-useful bias, with its looser techniques and more experimental ideas, incorporating curtain rings, wire and other objects not previously associated with embroidery. In fact the use of mixed media was becoming popular as were mixed techniques including the use of dyes, areas of fabric being painted, sprayed or dipped, instead of using appliqué to denote changes of colour. Machine embroidery merged well with these techniques and a more experimental attitude to embroidery was developing, not only among the art students but among the amateur executants.

The '62 Group's activities continued and in 1967 it held its first exhibition away from the Embroiderers' Guild premises, at the Festival Hall. In 1968 members showed work in Foyle's Art Gallery, their first exhibition in a public gallery, and in the spring of 1969 they exhibited at the Victoria and Albert Museum. Some of the shows went on tour with the Art Exhibitions Bureau. An interesting discussion among members arose from the exhibition of 1968, with some forthright criticisms being voiced. The conclusions were that little original work was shown, that good drawing was lacking in much of the work. The query 'What is good embroidery?' was answered rather vaguely: that it was 'design formed from a knowledge of basic elements composed with technical skill'. Some felt that embroidery in the 'fine art' area was no longer embroidery and required a new name and also asked 'why do embroiderers produce work?'. A more definite answer was 'to say something, to express an ideal'. The final thoughts were that embroidery should 'look like embroidery' but must be forward thinking, must be a personal means of expression, must retain its particular characteristics together with sound craftsmanship. (*Embroidery*, Volume XIX, Number 4, Winter 1968.)

The New Embroidery Group

In 1968 another group of embroiderers was founded, the New Embroidery Group, the nucleus being formed by some of the students who had attended part-time classes at Goldsmiths' School of Art before the Diploma in Art and Design commenced, after which they were no longer able to attend. The idea for the group was promoted by **Ione Dorrington** who was a technical assistant in the embroidery department and felt that there was a need for such a group which would encourage those without art backgrounds to pursue embroidery. The aim of this group was 'to exert a progressive influence and to produce a high standard of design and craftsmanship through the medium of embroidery and allied techniques'. It hoped, too, to hold exhibitions of members' work in different parts of the country.

Women's Institutes

As Women's Institutes promoted many crafts during this century a note on their organisation is appropriate as they did a great deal not only to promote the crafts but also to revive some of those in danger of dying out such as quilting and lacemaking. In 1920 they founded a Guild of Learners to develop interest in homecrafts, hoping to establish local cottage industries. This did not materialise but members of the Institutes were keen on increasing their own skills.

Various proficiency tests were begun and the first school was set up in Tunbridge Wells. Annual grants were given by the Development Commission and in the 1930s these schools were training instructors.

Amy Emms, a well-known quilter in Durham, began to work with the Women's Institutes in 1924 and organised classes for them throughout her area. These spread, providing some financial aid to the depressed coal mining districts. Through her the Rural Industries Bureau also provided financial help in reviving quilting in South Wales and the West of England.

Amy Emms was also instrumental in creating interest in smocking, having written a book on English smocking for Dryad in the 1930s.

From the early beginnings the WI have maintained their standards of craftsmanship. National exhibitions have been selected from local ones and have attracted many people. Home Economics certificates in judging and demonstrating are now given instead of those for the Guild of Learners.

Denman College, the Headquarters of the Women's Institutes, has promoted many courses for a number of crafts, and is continuing to do so.

Commercial enterprises

William Briggs and Co during and after the Second World War continued to produce yarns. The firm had produced packs for occupational therapy for hospital and service units, which formed a beginning of the traced linens and stencilled canvases with sets of threads provided for working them – which developed into the Penelope Tapestry Kits. In 1963 Frank Briggs, the Head of the firm, died; the business was liquidated but Messrs J and P Coats had a controlling interest in the firm. In December 1963 this was transferred to Eagley Mills, belonging to Coats, in Bolton. Colin Martin, the driving force of Coats from 1964 until his retirement, developed the resources of Briggs and in 1968 Penelope Needlework packs proved very successful, with a flourishing export trade. Although Briggs' identity as a firm disappeared its transfer to the older firm of Messrs Coats, with its connections and present-day methods, re-strengthened the original qualities of the annexed firm.

Other enterprises

Another enterprise, Arthur Lee's tapestry works in Birkenhead, which began in 1888, celebrated its seventieth anniversary in 1958, having become internationally known by this time. The business continued until December 1970 when it closed, having produced woven and embroidered works on a large scale. A great deal of hand embroidery was done including crewel work, surface stitchery and canvas work; also plain weaving and patterned tapestries on Jacquard looms, often with hand block printing of the tapestries, with many colours, over the weaving. From copying old embroideries the firm began to produce their own designs. They had a range of 240 colours from which to work and also used several different colours in one needle, thus obtaining subtle tones. Large murals in hand embroidery became a feature of the company. In 1930 they made a number of hangings for the Midland Bank Board Room and in 1964 the canvas mural for the Joint Matriculation Board Room in Manchester (4). By hand they produced curtains, carpets and seat covers in surface stitching or in canvas work. Subjects for design included floral and heraldic motifs as well as those for individual clients.

An exhibition at the Williamson Art Gallery and Museum, Birkenhead, marked the anniversary and in 1972 the Lee Tapestry Room was opened as a permanent record of the work and achievements of the company. (Information from *The Lee Tapestry Room*, Williamson Art Gallery and Museum, Birkenhead.) This has now been dismantled.

Experiment in embroidery

Valuable comments made in articles published in *Embroidery* during the sixties and seventies were thought-provoking with their stimulating and controversial points of view. Among the contributors, Kathleen Whyte talking about experiment said that 'it happened naturally' as embroidery was always changing. In the development of the craft she felt that the 'release of stitchery solely from pattern making to become a perfect drawing medium' was important and that there was now an interest in plant forms, rocks and stones. A reluctance in teaching stitchery was noticeable although there were many ways in which stitches could be presented to the student as 'something always new, fundamental, and to be used'. Ways of drawing were mentioned, one for investigation, preceding the embroidery, the other, the draughtsmanship and its quality as seen in the finished work. She felt that embroidery design should, ideally, have impact and grow more intriguing on closer inspection. She finalised her article by asking 'What is embroidery?' and saying that it is a 'synthesis of drawing, design, use of materials, colour and stitchery . . . they form a unity within which, by changing emphasis, all manner of expression and experiment is possible'. (*Embroidery*, Volume 15, Number 4, Winter 1964.)

Space was being recognised as a feature of design at the end of the fifties and now was becoming important in that a small, significant area of embroidery could be enhanced by space and that a background did not have to be filled with pattern. Remarks at some exhibitions such as 'what a waste of material' were heard, but gradually the discerning viewer began to appreciate the fact that clutter could dissipate the area of interest and the vitality of a design could be lost. An opposite approach was seen, too, in the mid-sixties lasting into the seventies with some embroiderers keen on the addition of extraneous objects to their stitchery such as wire, cardboard and plastic tubing and other plastic forms, stones, buttons, shells, nuts and bolts and other non-embroidery objects that quite frequently gave rise to gimmicky results, the bits and pieces having little or no connection with the fabrics and threads, unless incorporated by a skilled designer. This 'junk' embroidery grew partly from seeing work with applied objects used successfully by artists who understood what they were doing. It was also a desire to explore new possibilities that created surfaces with more depth. Without an understanding of design, the use of extraneous objects, coupled with indifferent technique, was often unsuccessful. Fortunately much of this phase, which was often accompanied by inferior technique, was short lived.

Audrey Tucker, who had obtained the National Diploma in Design at the Hammersmith College of Art and Building, wrote on 'Thoughts on the Future of Embroidery' in *Embroidery*, Volume 17, Number 1, Spring 1966. She said that 'we should be initiators of new images, concepts and inventive embroidery in order to influence other art forms. With the new Diploma in Art and Design there is a closer link with fine art'. She felt that students had a reluctance to link embroidery with stitches but that a revival of stitchery was imminent, also that an experimental stage was necessary using mixed media such as bric-a-brac, dyed and painted fabrics, as otherwise there was no progress. She felt, too, that a trend towards flat effects was apparent. The potential of the trade machines had not yet been realised as they had been used in imitation of hand embroidery or for drawing by students, and it was important that industry should be shown good, functional design. She wondered why the idea of studio embroidery had not been launched suggesting an embroidery industry on a competitive scale, as in pottery, and that the problem was in presenting a new and vital image.

A tendency already mentioned by Kathleen Whyte was noticed in colleges where young students were training for the Scottish Diploma in Art and for the National Diploma in Art and Design. This was a reluctance to use threads and stitches, resorting to the quicker method of fabric collage and a provocative but perceptive article by David Fletcher might be mentioned on this issue of designing for embroidery (*Embroidery*, Volume 15, Number 4, Winter 1964). He said that the students manipulated fabrics, added bits and pieces, but the addition of threads and stitches was often omitted, in other words they developed an aversion to embroidery. He said that circles and bark and cellular structures were in – they were universally used in Great Britain now – and that embellishment of useful articles had gone. Many ways of expressing themselves were used by artists, such as sculpture without clay, painting without paint and the attitude that 'anything goes' and unlimited freedom were a danger in art. He urged embroiderers in 'this period of bits and pieces' not to lose sight of the needle, not to 'lose sight of the aesthetics of embroidery'.

During the decade the word *collage* came into fashion as an alternative to appliqué, although its meaning was that of sticking fabrics or paper to a background instead of sewing them down. In the mid-sixties sticking fabrics was for a short time a speedy way of obtaining effects but this did not last long; however, the term began to be used for sewn appliqué with or without embroidery, students often obtaining livelier results by applying fabrics just caught down with plain stitching when trying out ideas, rather than by using embroidery with appliqué. Their reluctance to employ stitches, according to conversations with them, was that they did not wish their work to become 'stitchery stitchery', their expression for 'stitchery for stitchery's sake' instead of as a means of interpreting ideas and expressing personal thoughts.

Hand embroidery versus machine embroidery remained a matter of controversy among amateur stitchers during the sixties, the rise of commercial machine embroidery leading to 'a strong reaction from those who saw a threat to embroidery as they knew it'. Hand embroidery revived through this reaction, but prejudice against the domestic sewing machine as well as the industrial ones was strong. However, the Editor of *Embroidery* in Volume XX, Number 1, Spring 1969, felt that 'machine embroidered fabrics . . . no longer imitate hand embroidery but have developed on their own lines, stimulated by the demand from leading couturiers'. At this time machine embroidered fabrics from Europe were in fashion, imported from Switzerland and Italy. Hand embroidered garments were also in demand, often emphasised with beads.

Materials

Fabrics were now available in profusion, made entirely of natural fibres as well as mixtures of man-made and natural, or wholly man-made examples. The latter had improved in quality, although still lacking the pliability of the fabrics consisting of natural threads. Threads were also freely available, natural and man made, embroiderers finding that the man made were less easily manipulated, although stronger. Gold and silver kid and metal threads were very popular during the sixties, both for ecclesiastical and secular work. Experiments using plastic fabrics, both transparent and opaque, as well as imitation kid in gold and silver, were successful once their qualities, different from the real skins, were appreciated. Likewise, synthetic metal threads and lurex, specially made for machine embroidery, were useful if handled properly.

Dress

Bead embroidery became fashionable again during the sixties and in 1964 bead embroidered evening wear was seen in the spring collections of the London fashion designers. **Norman Hartnell**, well known for his lavish use of beads and embroidery, **Hardy Amies** and **John Cavanagh** among others, showed bead embroidered dresses which were in contrast to the simpler clothes seen for day wear. Machine embroidery was popular as it was durable, integrated well with fabric and was more speedy in application than hand embroidery so invaluable for work in the trade. In higher education garments were decorated in a variety of ways. The London College of Fashion had courses in hand embroidery, machine embroidery and beading, the beads applied to the fabric with a tambour hook. In **Stanley Lock**'s embroidery workrooms, his embroiderers used this method of applying beads to fabric (15), many of them now made of plastic as glass and china beads used in profusion could add considerable weight to garments. He carried out a great deal of work for the theatre and for television, as did other firms, and for individual stars, both men and women, who required eye-catching garments for appearances on the stage and the screen.

Zandra Rhodes and **Bill Gibb** among others, used embroidery with which to decorate their creations and by the end of the decade, really cheap clothes often embroidered, appealing to the young, were available in many of the boutiques that were springing up all over Britain. Men's clothes were now more colourful and the influence started by the Beatles was continued in the world of 'pop' music and entertainment, often with bizarre costumes heavily embroidered and sequined. Beaded garments of the twenties were sought after and by 1970 anyone could wear anything. The embroidered kaftan, which had been popular from the mid-sixties, continued in favour and ethnic garments from India, Afghanistan and the Near East, brought in by young travellers, started a craze for pattern with pattern and the layered look. The colleges of art, where dress and embroidery courses were held, often combined, and embroidery was carried out by students who studied both subjects, or students spent some time in each department so work could be interchanged. Ethnic garment shapes were copied or adapted, styles and patterns were often mixed and pieces of embroidery cut from worn garments were applied to new fabrics. The antique clothes market was born, and embroidered garments of the Victorian and Edwardian periods were sought after, as were lace-embellished clothes and the beaded gowns of the twenties.

Ecclesiastical embroidery

The sixties was a period of development of interest in embroidery for the Church and consequently an incentive for students to design and work embroidery for ecclesiastical purposes. Gold work was more popular than in the previous decade, metal threads, gold and silver kid and other colours being available to the embroiderer. Students became enthusiastic about the technique of *or nué* and a number of them carried out ecclesiastical examples using this method of work. See colour plate 12.

Several schemes of embroidery commenced at the end of the fifties were completed during the early sixties, among these the kneelers for the church of St Clement Danes, also the scheme for the kneelers and cushions for Eton College Chapel, begun in 1959 and finished in 1964.

All Hallows-in-the-Wall, London, by invitation of the Council for the Care of Churches, mounted an exhibition of contemporary ecclesiastical embroidery in the autumn of 1964. **Beryl Dean**'s cope and mitre for Guildford Cathedral, in plum-coloured silk and cloth of gold, was displayed, and among other exhibits was **Pat Russell**'s altar frontal with lettering. The show was opened by The Very Reverend Seiriol Evans MA, FSA, the Dean of Gloucester Cathedral, who gave some sound 'advice on' producing work for the Church, stressing the necessity for design. He felt that pictorial themes were unsuitable, that colour was important, as were symbolism and iconography, which should be understood by those who designed for ecclesiastical embroidery. (*Embroidery*, Volume 15, Number 4, Winter 1964.)

During the sixties professional and amateur embroiderers continued to work for the Church, in the conservation of old vestments and furnishings and by designing and carrying out new projects. Articles were written by artists and by churchmen on the recent 'breakthrough' of interest in ecclesiastical embroidery. Beryl Dean made some pertinent remarks in *Embroidery* Volume 15, Number 3, Autumn 1964, on the need for new, imaginative work, designed to suit the surroundings for which the embroidery was intended. She stressed the point that work on the continent of a contemporary style had been designed before the Second World War, but that much of the church embroidery in Great Britain was still very traditional, as was work produced by commercial firms. 'Uninspired products of the workrooms, where technique was more important than design, was the result of dull ideas by architects in Great Britain and of old-fashioned outlooks of the churchmen.' She felt that someone trained in another area of art, who defied convention but who knew the possibilities of the craft of embroidery, as a designer-executant, was the ideal required.

Lorna Tressider, teaching in Liverpool, produced an exhibition with her students to correspond with the opening of the new Roman Catholic Cathedral of Christ the King in Liverpool in May 1967. First- and second-year students on the Diploma course in dress and textiles produced many innovative ideas. The employment of unusual materials such as the use of safety pins for a complete design, the integration into a design of 'found' objects attached to the fabric in an imaginative way, and also the designing of vestments with shapes of an unconventional nature, gave practical experience invaluable to the students.

St Paul's Cathedral exhibition, 1968

The highlight of 1968, was the exhibition of ecclesiastical embroidery in May, in the crypt of St Paul's Cathedral. With the co-operation of staff and students from Goldsmiths' School of Art and Hammersmith College of Art and Building, **Beryl Dean**, whose idea it was, had worked hard to realise her vision in mounting a large show of contemporary ecclesiastical work, not previously brought together. Well-known artists loaned work, and students from colleges in various parts of the country contributed many pieces of embroidery, among these were small articles such as alms bags and burses. Larger examples included copes, altar frontals and throwovers as well as hangings and banners. Many of the designs were abstract with symbolic imagery (38). Metal threads, gold and silver kid, brilliantly coloured silks and woollen fabrics, as well as synthetics and plastics, were used for the embroideries, with an absence of the traditional brocades and damasks. Dyes were sometimes introduced and it was said that the general feeling was of rich and brilliant colour. Beryl Dean showed several embroideries, as did Pat Russell (9, 10, 11) and Barbara Dawson, while I exhibited a cope (40) in which synthetic threads and gold plastic were mixed with pure wools and silks. The cope, commenced in 1958 at the Hammersmith College of Art and Building, was now completed and, together with a mitre, was exhibited and donated to the Cathedral. See figures 28 and 29.

The show created enormous interest, its influence was far reaching and led to the formation of ecclesiastical embroidery classes in other parts of the country and to more churches commissioning work. St Andrew's Church, Holborn, staged the exhibition after its debut at St Paul's, again creating much interest. A greater concern for the conservation of old embroideries also stemmed from this exhibition.

The Reverend Doctor Gilbert Cope commenting on the work said that the show was an achievement but there should be more liaison between the artist and the client, that the briefing when commissioning work and the purpose and 'the form' of 'the article to be embroidered must be given great consideration, its state must suit its environment and designing for hangings and for vestments should be approached differently'. He quoted Nora Jones who said 'the fact that vestments are garments is often forgotten by priests and people'. He felt also that 'the eucharist vestments required a total reappraisal'. (*Embroidery*, Volume XIX, Number 3, Autumn 1968.)

In the Chapter House of York Minster, during the Festival of York in the summer of 1969, an exhibition of 'Church Embroidery and Handweaving' took place. A number of well-known embroiderers and students from colleges of art took part in the exhibition, which was a success, allowing those in the north of England to see the present-day trends in ecclesiastical work.

Jennifer Gray who had commenced designs for kneelers for Girton College Chapel, Cambridge, in 1962 saw their completion in 1969. They had been worked by past and present students, with designs adapted from early Christian art seen in the mosaics and low relief carvings in Ravenna and Rome. Different stitches were employed for variety and texture.

The interest in church embroidery continued throughout the decade, professional embroiderers designing and carrying out their ideas, while groups of women, often making their first attempts at embroidery, worked together to produce kneelers for their local places of worship. More ambitiously they embroidered frontals and banners and sometimes vestments.

Sylvia Green writing about her projects for the local church, St Michael's, Highgate, said that these drew together members of the congregation eager to be of service. Group meetings were held and experimental samplers made. For the first scheme, stall cushions, Sylvia Green drew simple shapes on graph paper to be interpreted on canvas differently by each member of the group. This allowed for the development of creativity and an individual choice of stitches, to her more important than the finished result. Colours, too, were chosen by members from a selection to complement the stained glass windows. The venture was successful and led to more projects. (*Embroidery*, Volume XXI, Number 1, Spring 1970.) During the early 1970s Sylvia Green designed vestments for the same church, including a red cope in Indian cotton (45, 46), for festivals, using applied fabrics with a minimum of stitchery.

Designs for the larger examples were often given as commissions to artists among whom were painters and weavers, the embroidery then being executed by the groups, under the guidance of an expert in ecclesiastical embroidery. Latitude for an individual choice of stitches or an arrangement of motifs, with co-ordinated colours, was a way of avoiding monotony and often a part of the scheme when kneelers were being worked by groups, this giving some outlet for personal expression.

Commemorative embroidery

Embroidery was sometimes a means of commemoration as were the mourning pictures of the early nineteenth century. These were individual pieces or executed by groups of embroiderers, both amateur and professional, as communal projects. Works were undertaken in memory of a particular event or of a person.

The Hastings Tapestry

An example of a commemorative piece of work is the so-called '*Hastings Tapestry*', with an explanation in the foreword to the catalogue indicating that it is not a tapestry but an embroidery. This embroidery was commissioned by the Hastings Borough Council to show the most important happenings that have affected Britain over the last 900 years, and to mark the Battle of Hastings in 1066. The idea was thought of as a present-day version of the Bayeux Tapestry and was carried out by the Royal School of Needlework, commencing on 1 July 1965. It was divided into 27 panels, each 9 ft wide by 3ft high (2.74 m by 91 cm), mounted on stretchers and worked in appliqué, in cords, metals and other threads. Subjects were chosen after consultation with experts in art and history, references being obtained from Royal Palaces, museums, books and private sources. The result is a pictorial history on a large scale and is housed in the Tridome, a building specially commissioned to contain the Hastings Tapestry which was completed within the year, ready for the commemorative celebrations. (*The Hastings Embroidery*, The Tridome souvenir catalogue.)

The opening of the Tay Bridge

The opening of the Tay Bridge on 18 August 1966 by Queen Elizabeth, the Queen Mother, was commemorated by a presentation to her of an embroidered stole worked by Kathleen Whyte on silk handwoven by Ursula Brock. See figure 21.

Embroiderers in the sixties

Margaret Nicholson and **Beryl Dean** were teaching at the Embroiderers' Guild in 1964–65. **Jan Beaney** became a lecturer in art in a training college in 1964 as did **Rosalind Floyd** in 1965, while **Jane Page** in 1964 started as a full time lecturer in embroidery at Derby College of Art, and **Crissie White** in Dundee College of Art was appointed to take charge of embroidery and weaving. In 1965 **Dorothy Reglar** commenced work in an embroidery workroom to design and organise the work for Belville Sassoon.

Hanna Frew Paterson in 1968 taught in the embroidery department of the Glasgow School of Art as a full-time assistant. **Mary Ward**, too, taught there part time. **Diana Springall** started to teach in a college of education as did **Richard Box**, in 1968. **Alison Liley** became Head of textiles/fashion at Derby College of Art, while **Patricia Beese** left the West of England College of Art to take charge of embroidery at Loughborough College of Art and Design.

Early in 1966 a remarkable exhibition was arranged at the Crane Kalman Gallery in London, of 60 works by **Elizabeth Allen**, an 82-year old lady who had been 'discovered' by an art student, Bridget Poole, in 1964. She had been living in a hut in a wood in Kent where she had barely existed since 1935. Through the student's care, Elizabeth Allen, known as 'Queenie', was able to continue with her very personal work. Patrick Heron, in the preface to the catalogue of her first exhibition said that he was 'utterly carried away by the magical beauty and profundity of her pictures', which were all in rag and sewn invisibly unless lines were required. The subjects were biblical or secular, the earlier work showing a more linear style which had gradually changed through the years to areas of pure colour, the fabrics fitting together like mosaic, with lines only for emphasis (16). Subjects were completely pictorial, often fantasy, and all had titles such as *Mary at the Tomb* and *Christ Before Pilate*, or *Flowers in a Vase* and *Good-bye Mum, off to Church*. The tonal qualities were excellent and the simplification of figures and objects to flat silhouettes of colour seemed dateless although the costume was from the 1920s onwards. (Information from the Catalogue, Crane Kalman Gallery, February–March 1966.)

Another embroiderer was praised by Marina Vaizey, the art critic for several publications, who said in 1967 in *Arts Review*: '**Eugenie Alexander** has been a pioneer in the field of fabric collages and her pictures are deservedly well-known. Some are meticulously designed, others show her talent for exhuberant decoration, and her work allies an element of fantasy to a vigorous and robust sense of colour. . . . She is achieving . . . an exploration of depth, technically by means of overlapping layers of net and gauze, that provides an imaginative realisation in fabrics – of the effects that are sometimes achieved in watercolours. This is an art form in itself of surprising richness'. See figure 24 and colour plate 6.

Sheila Ashby, originally a painter, studied embroidery part time in evening classes at Glasgow School of Art. Since living in the USA she has studied needlelace with Virginia Bath. She teaches embroidery and brings groups to England to study the subject. See figure 121.

Jan Beaney trained as a painter but began to embroider on the Art Teachers' Certificate course at Hornsey College of Art with Eirian Short. She taught embroidery to children and then to adults. Her work is based on careful drawings of things seen in her environment; landscape, gardens, plants and trees have a particular appeal for her and are a source of much of her design.

Anne Butler taught at Goldsmiths' School of Art for a few years. She carried out a number of commissions during this time, mainly ecclesiastical; her style of work being geometric, using hand and machine techniques.

Julia Caprara first embroidered in 1969, finding that she was interested in surfaces and contrasting textures. Her training enabled her to work on small to large-scale ideas and many of her early examples consisted of textures in different threads with stitches piled on stitches, cloth wrinkled up and ends of threads often left hanging. She was inspired by nature and landscape and through these studies, said that 'I became aware of parallels with symbolic ideas . . . of the unconscious in mythology'.

Elspeth Crawford continued to paint and to embroider during the sixties, teaching also at Grays School of Art, Aberdeen, until 1966. She held a number of exhibitions of mixed media, painting and embroidery, and is still influenced by the patterns and colours of peasant and primitive art. See figures 116, 141, 142.

Ione Dorrington started to embroider during the early sixties having attended a day course at the Embroiderers' Guild. She attended part-time classes at Goldsmiths' School of Art where she studied for Part I of the City and Guilds examination in embroidery. Her design was often geometric but she carried out quite varied experiments to find out what could be done with stitches. See figure 42.

Joyce Conwy Evans trained as an embroiderer and a weaver, but having a versatile approach to work, designed costumes for Glyndebourne and worked with Sir Hugh Casson, collaborating with him on such projects as the renovation of the Royal Albert Hall and Christmas decorations for Regent Street. She saw embroidery for interior design, rather than for small pieces of work. She designed embroidery for the academic robes of the Royal College of Art in 1967, worked by Elizabeth Geddes. See figure 34.

Patricia Foulds continued during the sixties to teach in Bristol, where she developed embroidery with fashion students. In 1968 she was appointed to take charge of the diploma course in art and design in embroidery, at Loughborough College of Art and Design, where she says 'I have become more interested in the breadth of the subject'.

Janet Graham, originally an illustrator, worked part time in order to continue her training, also part time, as an embroiderer. She taught some classes at Goldsmiths' School of Art and in several other places. She exhibited in various galleries and carried out some ecclesiastical commissions during the decade. Her work was mainly for wall decorations, quite freely designed, combining hand and machine techniques and mixing swirling curves with straight lines that gave movement to her ideas. See figure 22.

Sylvia Green in 1965 founded the St Michael's Embroidery Group at Highgate. This flourished and vestments, kneelers and frontals were designed by her and carried out by herself and the Group, for St Michael's Highgate and then for other buildings. See figures 39, 45, 46, 147 and 148.

Maureen Helsdon held a one-man show at the Crafts Centre of Great Britain in 1965, also exhibiting at Southampton University.

Diana Jones from an anathema to canvas work and patchwork, changed her mind in the early sixties. She decided that design could grow from the colours and textures of yarns and she produced work with the background covered entirely with stitches. This led to canvas work; a technique with which she has continued.

Alison Liley in 1965 talking on the scope of flowers used in embroidery said that 'they translate into delicate design' and that 'there is a present feeling for free, spontaneous lively drawing, with irregularity of pattern and shape'.

Dorothy Reglar (née Darch), after a post-diploma course at Birmingham College of Art and Design in 1966, worked for some time as an embroidery designer at Belville Sassoon. She then became a freelance fashion designer, also teaching part time in Hornsey College of Art. In the early seventies she was interested particularly in designing clothes for children.

Pat Russell, since starting her work with fabrics in 1960, has carried out a number of collages and machine stitched ecclesiastical vestments, hangings and frontals (9, 10). She wanted to design large embroideries and required the challenge of a particular environment. Machine embroidery was speedier than hand embroidery for her, but was used mainly as a means of attaching fabrics to a background. As her training was in calligraphy some of her work involved lettering, examples of which are illustrated. See figures 10 and 11.

Lilla Speir continued to design and carry out embroidery for hangings and smaller pieces of work during the sixties and the early seventies. She was a full-time lecturer in charge of embroidery at Manchester College of Art, now Manchester Polytechnic, which was selected for the Diploma in Art and Design in the early part of the decade. From Manchester she went to Belfast School of Art as Head of Embroidery. See figure 64 and colour plate 7.

Marion Stewart concentrated in the sixties on pictorial embroidery, using surface stitchery and appliqué. Her later work was more formalised, with less fluid, geometric shapes. See figure 18.

Margaret Traherne continued to paint and to design stained glass and textiles, exhibiting work in a number of places including the Whitechapel Gallery, the Tate Gallery and with the London Group. In 1966 she represented Great Britain at the Commonwealth Art Treasures exhibition at Burlington House. She began to create banners and flags for public buildings later on.

Lorna Tressider (née Derbyshire), a painter who first studied embroidery on the Art Teachers' Certificate course at Goldsmiths' College, had always been interested in needlework. She said that 'Constance Howard has had the greatest influence on my career. I was also taught machine embroidery by Christine Risley . . . Constance Howard saw embroidery as an art, a high and excellent art that it had held in past times'.

After some part-time teaching in Liverpool College of Art, she was appointed as a senior lecturer. See figures 100 and 101.

Crissie White said that during the sixties she felt that there was a strong Scandinavian influence in embroidery, but also the possibilities of economic expansion. In her own work she carried out hand embroidery and collage, but later developed an interest in small tapestries, canvas work (132) and patchwork (169). Fabrics such as silk, familiar to staff teaching before the Second World War, she felt were a new and inspiring basis of ideas for post-war students, so a degree of freshness was available to students with these 'new' materials.

Anna Wilson began to embroider during the early sixties and realised that she had an aptitude for the craft, finding it easy to use the right stitches for what she wanted to express, but starting with domestic articles she advanced to wall hangings, producing a number of larger pieces of work. See figure 117.

Design trends in the late sixties

There was a continued interest in abstract and geometric pattern in the late sixties. Landscape, figurative compositions and 'pop art' were sources of ideas with the copying of black-and-white newspaper photographs and others which were beginning to attract attention. The importance of space was emphasised further and the vignette-like arrangements in the designs of the fifties had disappeared, compositions often extending up to or over the frames or to the edges of the materials. A definite advance in ideas and in the standards of design was apparent on the diploma courses with the greater freedom given to the colleges of art to devise their own individual syllabuses. Large hangings, small framed pieces as well as canvas embroideries were produced for wall decoration; dress embroidery was worked on both domestic and industrial machines. Cellular structures, bark, the exploded circle and other geometric forms were still a basis of design for many of the embroiderers. The employment of mixed media was prevalent with dyes sprayed, painted and printed on to fabrics, tying and dyeing, batik and resist dyeing of fabrics before they were embroidered, giving an added depth to the final work. Experiment was encouraged: chicken-wire, plastics both rigid and pliable were worked into or applied to fabrics. Rags, beads and plastic strings were used and gold and silver pliable plastic fabrics, already mentioned, continued as substitutes for kid in some ecclesiastical embroidery, along with the synthetic metal threads, sometimes these imitations producing interesting results. Quilted and padded forms were a prelude to soft sculpture.

Embroidery at the end of the sixties

Collage, with or without embroidery, continued to intrigue students and embroidery on dress remained much in evidence at the end of the sixties, while three-dimensional forms and padded relief embroideries became popular. Machine embroidery vied with hand embroidery for precedence. The craze for photographic images, often copies in black-and-white, continued into the early seventies. A more realistic approach in both painting and embroidery was noticeable, portraits of the Queen and famous film stars appeared in canvas stitchery or in appliqué. Students taking diploma courses studied photography, often making direct translations into fabric and threads from the images taken, thus avoiding drawing and design.

Now sculptors and painters were using rags, clay and paint among other media; embroiderers added metal, clay and other non-embroidery materials to their repertoire, sometimes the mixing of materials and techniques producing lively, unexpected results. Styles were changing with semi-abstraction and geometric pattern intermingled. Landscape became a favourite subject in the early seventies, having been of interest to students during the late sixties. For some time food had been a theme for imitation in clay and now began to appear in fabric and stitchery, as flat pattern, in relief and padded, or three dimensionally, sometimes in life-like size, sometimes much larger or smaller in scale. Fried eggs made of silks in black velvet pans, birthday and wedding cakes in white satin and velvet, with silver beads and embroidered decoration, plum cakes too, filled with jet beads, wooden beads and small buttons were surprisingly realistic, as were open sandwiches with a multitude of fillings on brown foam-rubber 'Danish bread', embroidered by hand and machine (85). Fish, sausages and vegetables such as dyed cotton leeks and velvet carrots appeared. Huge liquorice allsorts as cushions were seen in more than one college, these sweets having a strong decorative appeal. The soft sculpture craze developed during the early seventies. This was probably through the work of painters who, in their turn, were influenced by 'pop' ideas, Claes Oldenburg being one of the prime instigators of 'soft art'. In the USA he produced the soft drainpipe, the soft telephone and the soft typewriter during the 1960s. With renewed interest in figurative work some life-sized fabric sculptures of figures were seen, built up on chicken-wire or wire structures. Large pieces of work such as decorated tents, units put together to make wall hangings on a bigger scale, hangings painted with dye, with some stitchery as emphasis, particularly those based on landscape, continued in popularity. Screenprinting with embroidery was another development, where stitch and print were often mingled and from a distance were indistinguishable, paper collage mixed with fabric was also seen.

Art courses in the late sixties

More drawing was evident in colleges, and on courses students were keen to draw, a reversal of the attitude in the mid-sixties already mentioned when drawing was often avoided or thought of as unnecessary if photography was used as a substitute. With a revaluation of drawing and a keenness to experiment on paper with design and colour, there was a consequent raising of standards with more successful practical results from a certain amount of planning. Exhibitions of diploma work in the colleges of art and in the polytechnics helped to increase current appreciation. Experimental samples were often exhibited as well as completed embroideries and sketch books containing written notes, scraps of fabric and alternative ideas on problems set, drawings, newspaper and magazine cuttings, paper collage, in fact anything that was useful to record for future reference. Sheets of design and drawings accompanying practical work always created lively interest. These displays were open to the public and proved to be stimulating and often controversial.

Articles on the structures of these courses as well as on others were written by heads of departments and by students. The students wrote about the work that they had produced for their diplomas, on their aims in creating particular examples, these were illustrated by photographs. All of these articles helped to give a picture of the development of embroidery towards the end of the sixties and throughout the next decade, a number being published in *Embroidery*. The magazine also contained descriptions and illustrations of work by professional artists and embroiderers, showing a diversity of styles and techniques.

Books

During the 1960s books on embroidery multiplied, both here and also in the USA. Some contained lively, innovative ideas, others reflected what had been written previously. As the interest in embroidery increased so did the number of publications, with 'how to do it' books dominating rather than those concerned with the aesthetics of design and an appreciation of the craft.

2 1964 – Jan Herman. A panel based on a cross section of a plant stem. The background is brown poult, with hand and machine stitching. Natural wood shavings are applied, also pebbles secured with net; canvas, raffia cloth and scrim are also used. *The Embroiderers' Guild Collection. Photograph loaned by the Embroiderers' Guild*

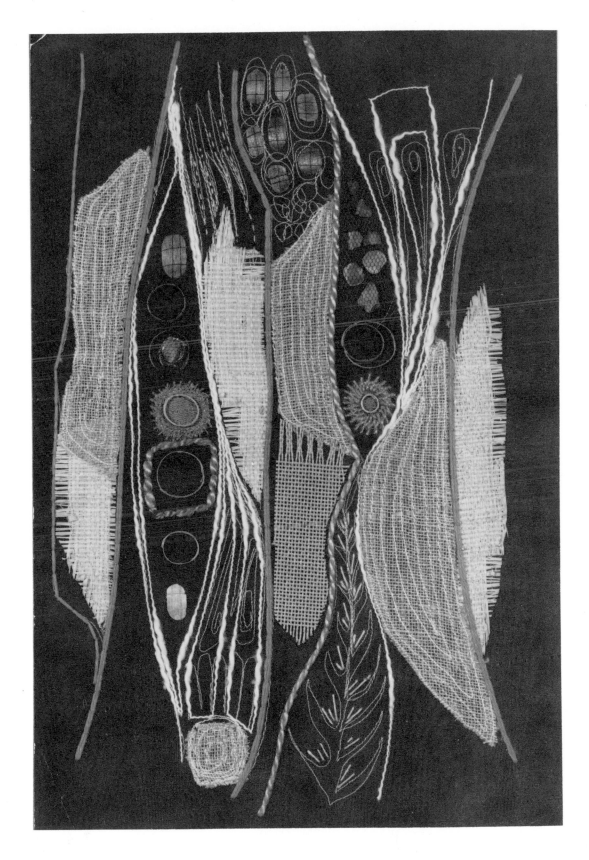

3 1964 – Sadie Allen. *Village Street Hethersgill,* **24 in.** × **36 in. (61 cm** × **91 cm).** Appliqué in a variety of fabrics including nets, chiffons, wool and cotton, with hand stitchery

4 Above right: 1964 – Stephen Lee. *Minerva,* **32 ft** × **7 ft 8 in. (9.75 m** × **2.34 m).** Designed by Stephen Lee and worked in wools on canvas; handstitching by the firm of Arthur Lee and Sons Limited. *In the Board Room of the Joint Matriculation Board, Manchester*

5 Right: 1964 – Stephen Lee *Minerva.* **A detail**

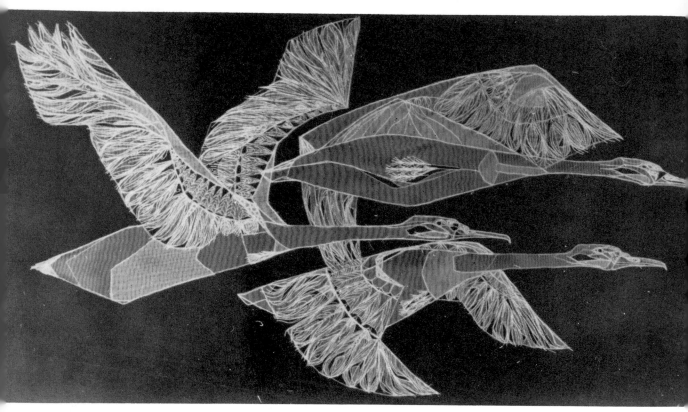

6 1964 – Audrey Tucker. *Flying Swans.* **Machine embroidery in white on layers of white nylon.** *Private collection, Australia*

7 Right: 1964 – Pat Ross. A student at Glasgow School of art. *Seagull,* **24 in. × 30 in. (61 cm × 76 cm). In linen, nets and pieces of different textures of material, in contrasts of rough and smooth, closely and openly woven. A variety of stitches in different yarns unifies the whole idea**

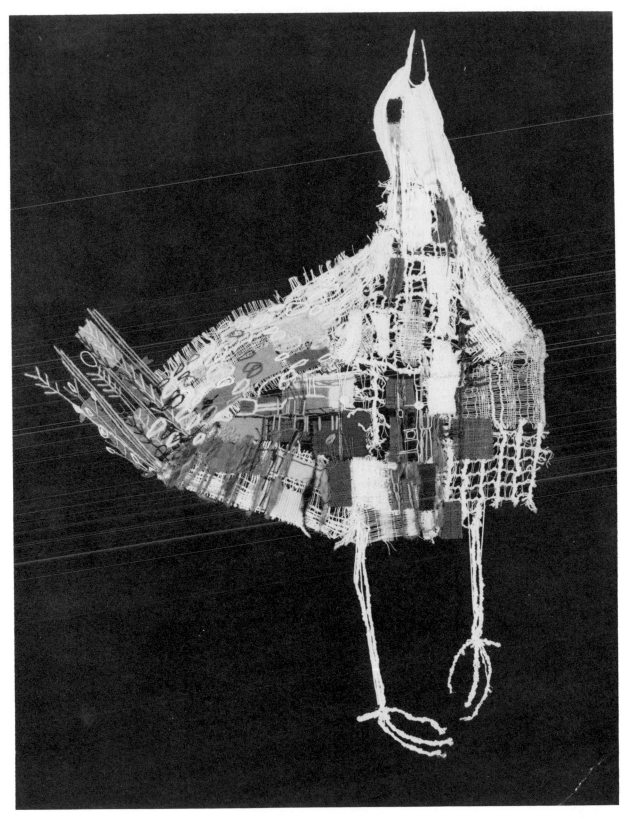

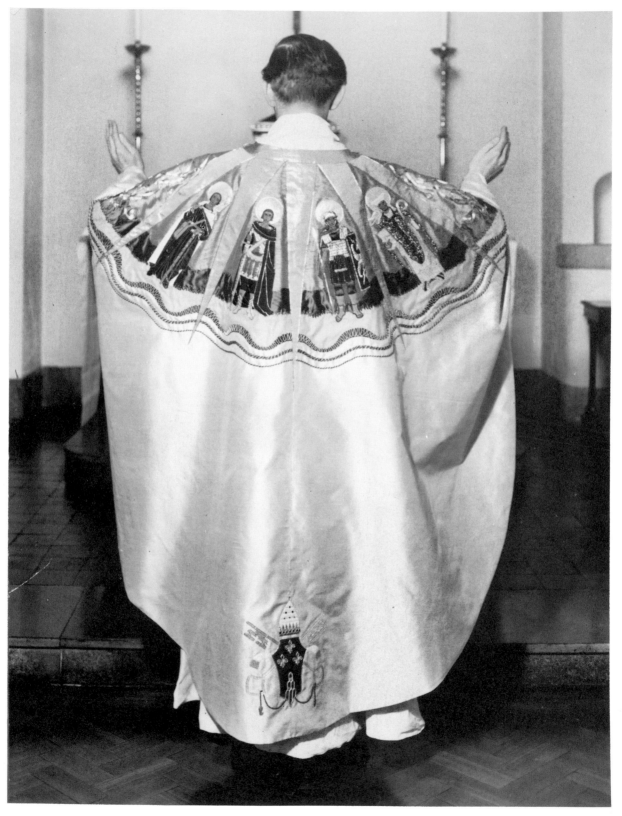

8 Left: 1965 – Sister Kathleen. The design for the cope by Laurence King FRIBA, worked by Sister Kathleen; made for Pope Paul VI. The background is cream wild silk, the rays in gold lurex lamé. The background behind the saints is blue. The saints are St Columba, St Alban, St George and St David – Celtic saints pre-597 AD. The waves represent the sea lapping the shores of Great Britain and are in blue and aluminium cord. The shores are greeny sandy organza with dark green fields behind

9 1965-66 – Pat Russell. A frontal for the High Altar, Pershore Abbey. Made in a variety of fabrics, with three crowns in gold kid. Machine stitchery. *Photograph by M F Couchman*

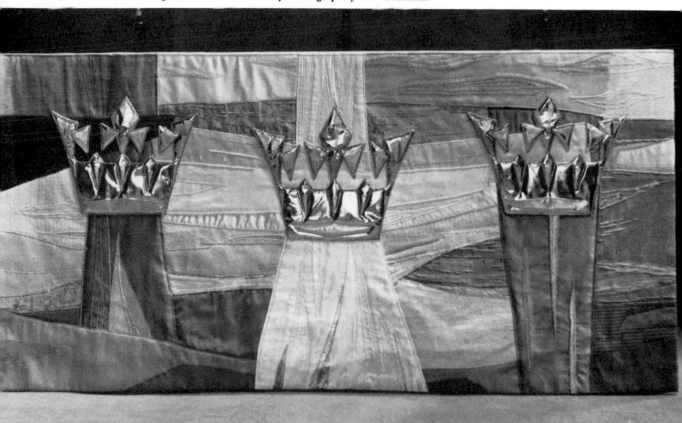

10 1965 – Pat Russell. Frontal, 72 in. × 36 in. (183 cm × 91 cm), for Pershore Abbey in the Chapel of St Edburgha who 'forsook the world for the book and the chalice'.
Photograph by R B Fleming and Co Ltd

11 Right: 1967 – Pat Russell. A stole in applied fabrics and machine embroidery. The words read 'Take my yoke upon you and learn of me'

12 Above: 1965 – Hebe Cox. *Seabirds*, 25 in. × 19½ in. (63.5 cm × 49.5 cm).
The stitching is in wools in greys, pinks, purple, black and white.
Photograph by Commercial Studios

13 Left: 1965-66 – Ann Mary Pilcher. Leather box decorated in couched
metal thread, beads and sequins. *Photograph loaned by the Embroiderers'
Guild*

14 Right: 1966 – Vera Sherman. *Cock*. A fabric collage in a variety of
textures. *Exhibited with 'Contemporary Hangings', 1966*

36

16 Above: Elizabeth Allen. *Babylon Riding on the Great Red Dragon.* **Shown at the exhibition at the Crane Kalman Galleries in 1966. The work was executed during the 1920s but not discovered until the 1960s. Most of the exhibits were biblical in nature, with applied fabrics and stitching to give lines dividing areas**

15 Left: 1960s – Stanley W Lock. A bead sample of 'daisies' for the trade. Yellow raffia, yellow-green leaves, silver centres of the flowers and a silver edging. Worked on transparent nylon. *Photograph by Hawkley Studios*

17 1965 – Audrey Tucker. *Old Woman with a Bird*. Hand and machine embroidery on a background of purple hessian. The figure is in black wools, the bird in gold and purple with gold beads

18 Mid-1960s – Marion Stewart. *St George and the Dragon.* **Hand embroidery using various stitches and materials**

19 1966 – Joan Cleaver. A dossal worked under the supervision of Joan Cleaver at Birmingham Polytechnic by the staff and students. The dossal was shown at the Church of England Pavilion Agricultural Show.

20 Right: 1966 – Joan Cleaver. A detail of the dossal worked at the Birmingham Polytechnic

21 1966 – Kathleen Whyte. A stole, commissioned by Dundee Corporation, for presentation to Her Majesty Queen Elizabeth, The Queen Mother, on the opening of the Tay Bridge in Scotland. The fabric in cream and gold was woven by hand by Ursula Brock. The embroidery is in gold thread and river pearls (found in the mussels in the Tay). The three emblems repesent the County of Angus (a crowned heart), the City of Dundee (a vase of lilies) and Fife (a knight on a charger). *Owned by Queen Elizabeth, The Queen Mother*

22 Far right: Mid-1960s – Janet Graham. A hand-embroidered panel approximately 34 in. × 22 in. (86.5 cm × 56 cm) in silks, with metal thread and silk thread. The main colours are yellows, creams and orange

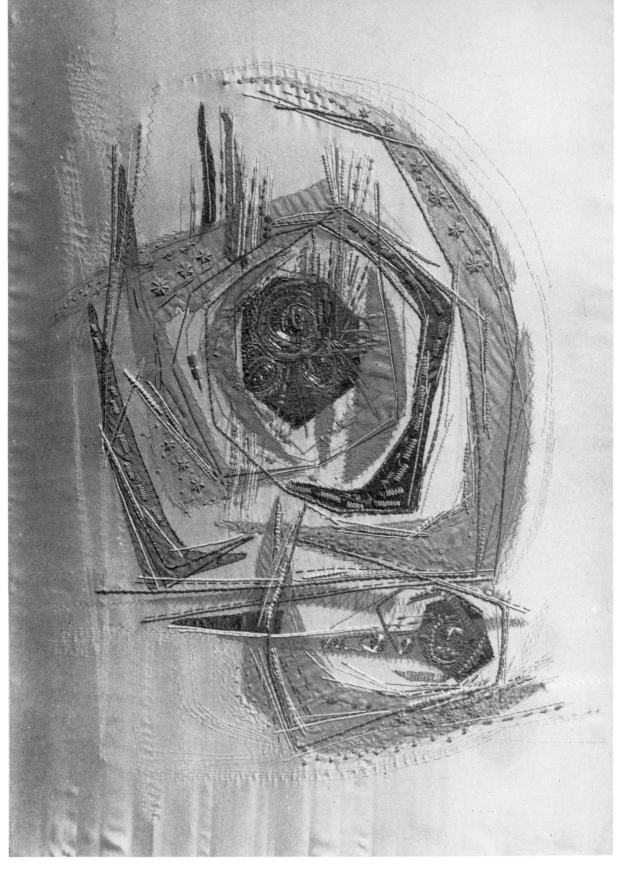

23 Mid-1960s – Moyra McNeil. A panel in aluminous gauze, partly covered by canvas stitches. The design is based on an electrical circuit. *The Victoria and Albert Museum Collection*

24 Right: 1966 – Eugenie Alexander. *Blue Monkey*, **40 in. × 56 in. (101.5 cm × 142 cm). Felt and other fabrics applied to a fabric ground.** *Photograph by John Hunnex*

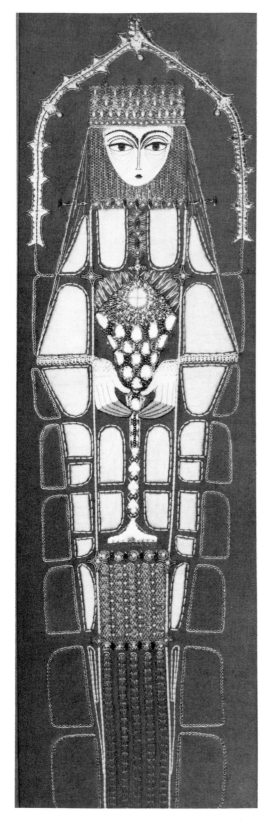

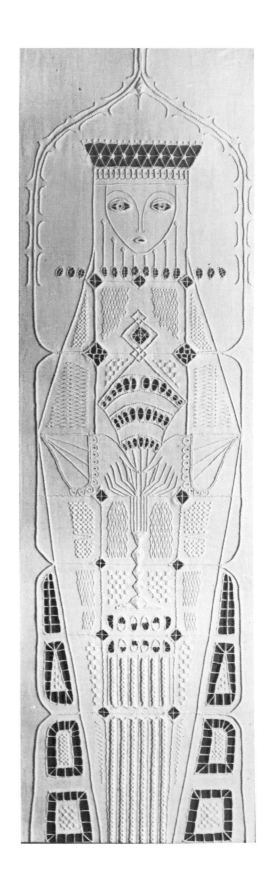

1966 – Margaret Nicholson. *St Clare of Assisi*, the patron saint of embroiderers. Designed as a contribution to the Diamond Jubilee. Eight versions were worked by different volunteers in a variety of techniques. The symbol in the hands – a monstrance – is changeable to suit any saint. The three photographs shown are:

25 Far left: Barbara Manning. Khaki face cloth with a variety of turquoise silks, blind appliqué, with the monstrance in padded gold kid, beads and pearls

26 Centre left: Mrs Crookes. Cut work, embroidered in raised stitches on white linen

27 Left: Susanna Pearson. The background is apricot silk with surface stitches in dark colours, including purples

**28 1958-67. The Hammersmith cope, a
community project designed by Susan
Riley and worked by members of the
ecclesiastical embroidery class at
Hammersmith College of Art and
Building. Machine and hand embroidery
on a dark red ground. Saints with
symbols were worked by individual
members.** *Photograph by Thomas
Simmons*

**29 Far right: 1958-67. A detail of the
Hammersmith cope, showing St Peter
with a key.** *Photograph by Thomas
Simmons*

30 Left: 1958-67 – A front view of the Hammersmith mitre showing St Paul; worked in couched gold thread. The background is red, the robe in a lighter red fabric.
Photograph by Thomas Simmons

31 Left: 1967 – George Pace. A dalmatic designed for St Alban's Abbey and worked by Mary Ozanne. The design is cut on the lines of an ancient style. The St Alban's cross is at the top of the garment, the large oval at the bottom is one of three, one on the chasuble and one on the tunicle. This stresses the hierarchical inter-relationships of the Celebrant, Deacon and Sub-Deacon. The remaining pattern is abstract. Lurex cord and braid are used for the embroidery. *Photograph by A C Thatcher and loaned by the Embroiderers' Guild*

32 Above: 1966-67 – A photograph of Diploma students at Goldsmiths' School of Art working on Barbara Dawson's red and scarlet cope, burse and veil: Carol Jackson, Verina Warren (née Jones), Diane Bates, Susan Weildon

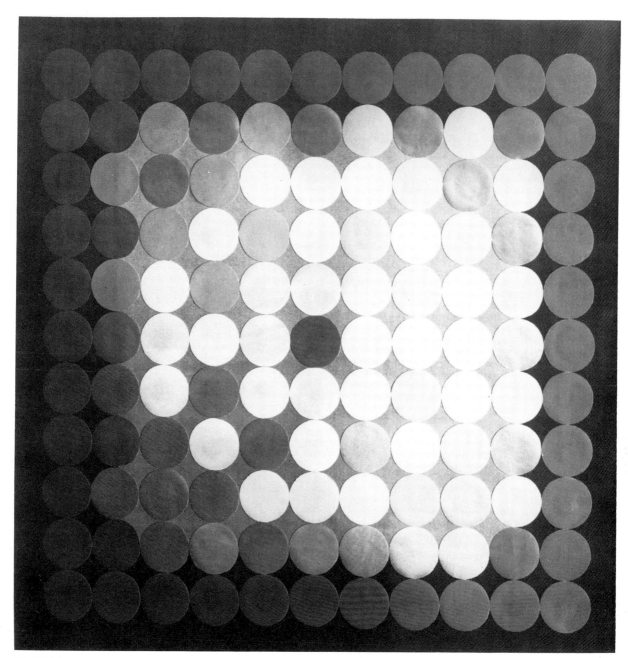

33 1966-67 – Jennifer Gray. *Growing Jade.* In applied shot silk fabric. The change in direction of weave of the circles and the light upon them gives an apparent movement when seen from different angles, the colours changing accordingly. *Exhibited with the '62 Group travelling show. Photograph loaned by the Embroiderers' Guild*

34 Right: 1967 – Joyce Conwy Evans. Ceremonial robes for the Royal College of Art, using the crowned phoenix emblem of the College on the Provost's collar and adapting the flame pattern from this to form the facings and sleeve motifs. The enrichments are tapestry, woven by the Edinburgh Tapestry Company in gold and silver threads. Gold and silver embroidery is by Elizabeth Geddes and two assistants. The robes are in black silk made by Ryder and Amies, Cambridge. The painting in the photograph is by Sir Robin Darwin, Rector of the Royal College of Art, of Professor Robert Gooden, in the robes of the Pro-Rector

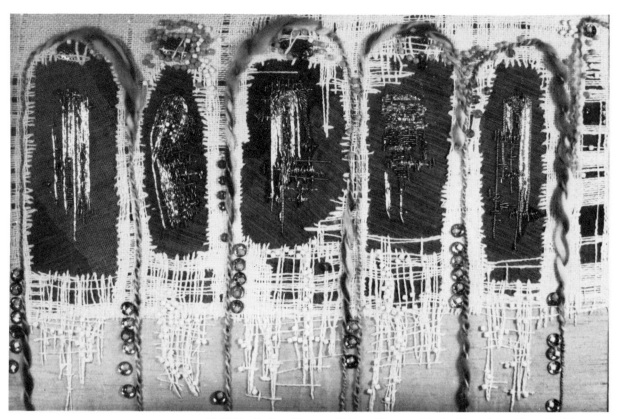

35 1967 – Barbara Dawson. *Pallaza.* **The ground is sky blue fabric with appliqué in coarse white linen, frayed. Fawn fabric and gold kid are applied. Gold thread, silk and beads, with some sequins, complete the work**

36 1967 – Jose Barnes. Student at Goldsmiths' School of Art taking the NDAD in embroidery. A head in canvas work, 12 in. × 9 in. (30.5 cm × 23 cm). Looped and flat stitches in a variety of threads, in pinks, dark reds and yellows

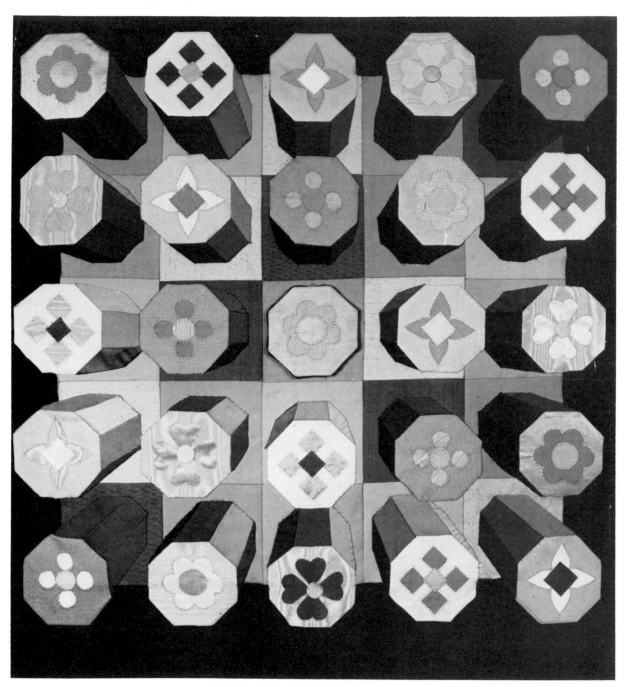

37 1967 – Eirian Short. *Projection.* **A completely flat panel 30 in. (76 cm) square with vanishing point perspective and tones distributed to create light and shade, giving an effect of three-dimensional forms projecting from the background. Colours are brilliant red, green, turquoise, pink, yellow and orange.** *Photograph by John Minchell*

38 1968 – Eirian Short. *The Creation.* A patchwork, 6 ft (183 cm) square, in a jigsaw technique, each shape covered in fabric and fitted together. The panel was made for the exhibition in St Paul's Cathedral Crypt in 1968. *Photograph by John Minchell*

39 1968 – Sylvia Green and Mary Hall. *The City.* **A choir-stall cushion for St Michael's Church, Highgate. Designed by Sylvia Green and embroidered on canvas by Mary Hall in a variety of stitches. Colours are gold, purple and red on a drab green background.**
Photograph by John Gay

40 Right: 1968 – Constance Howard. A cope on an orange Welsh flannel background. The cream circles are in thick silk, the gold and silver padded areas are in plastic fabric. The threads are entirely in synthetic gold and silver, with some aluminium, couched down with silk. One of the reasons for using synthetic threads and plastic fabrics was to find out their wearing qualities

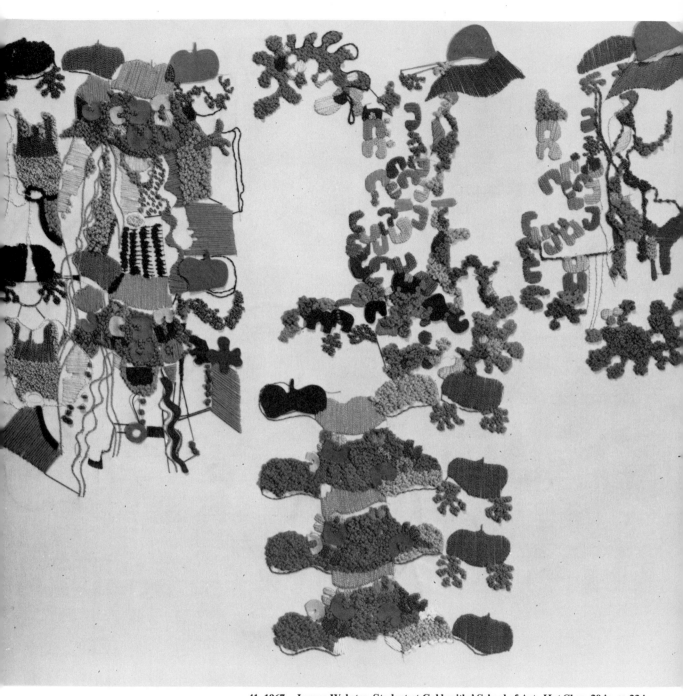

41 1967 – Joanne Webster. Student at Goldsmiths' School of Art. *Hat Shop*, 20 in. × 23 in. (51 cm × 58.5 cm). An appliqué in felt, silks and other fabrics on a white cotton background, in brilliant pinks, orange, yellow, blue and red. Hand stitching with french knots, straight stitches, back stitch and couching

42 Late 1960s – Ione Dorrington. A patchwork roundel 7½ in. (19 cm) in diameter. Colours are grey, blues and mauves

43 1960s – Kenneth Dow Barker. *Two Sheep.* **Grey-white sheep with figures in black, grey and tan. All in darning stitch. An illustration to** *Stitch and Stone.* *By courtesy of Audrey Barker, published by the Ceolfrith Press, Sunderland*

44 1960s – Kenneth Dow Barker. *Cattle at Kentmere.* **Black and white cows in green landscape. All in darning stitch. An illustration to** *Stitch and Stone.* **By courtesy of Audrey Barker, published by the Ceolfrith Press, Sunderland**

45 1969 – Sylvia Green. A cope
designed and made by Sylvia Green. Red
handwoven Indian cotton, with the
symbol of the Eucharist Angel in
appliqué, in pink, rose, wine and gold
silks; gold kid, jap gold and other silk
threads are also used. *Belonging to the
Prebendary Harry Edwards.
Photograph by John Gay*

46 Far right: 1969 – Sylvia Green.
Detail of cope

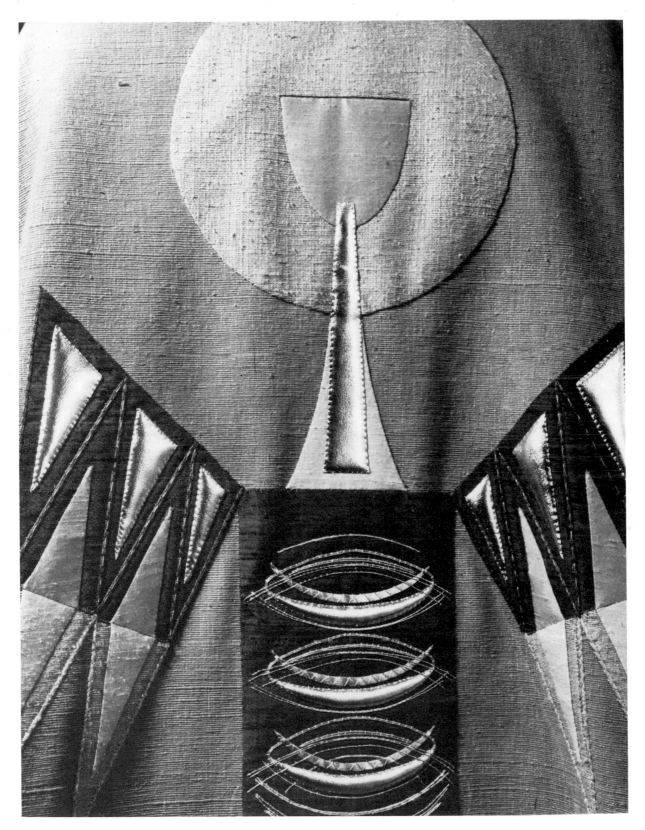

47 Left: 1969 – Beryl Dean. *The Burning Bush,* **39 in. × 10 ft (99 cm × 305 cm). A frontal for St Margaret's Church, King's Lynn. In applied fabrics in tones of red. A variety of textures are used for the embroidery**

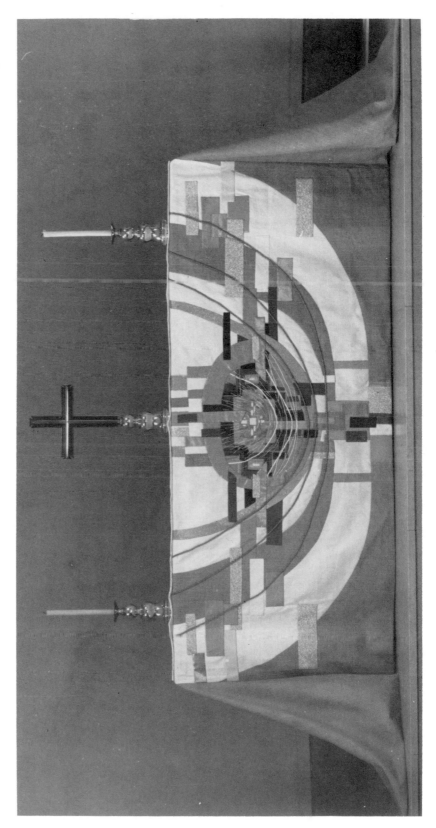

48 1969 – Barbara Dawson. A white laudian for Downing College, Cambridge, in metal thread and applied fabrics

49 1969 – Isabel Clover. A burse, 8 in. (20 cm) square. A rose embodying a cross, symbolic of the Virgin and Child. The cross is in gold fingering in Roman stitch and gold thread. Padded pewter kid, gold, coral and antique gold cord, buttonholed over string, are also used. The centre is raised and padded and covered with pearls, kid and satin stitch. *Owned by The Reverend B Peter. Photograph by M Saunders*

50 Right: 1969 – Lesley Hogger, a pupil at Dalston County Secondary School and winner of the Embroiderers' Guild Schools Challenge Cup, advanced section. *Oodles*, a panel 22½ in. × 27½ in. (57 cm × 70 cm), worked in white, off white and natural wools on a natural hessian ground, with couching and french knots, covered card rings, some held in place with woven wheels and raised satin stitch. *Photograph loaned by the Embroiderers' Guild*

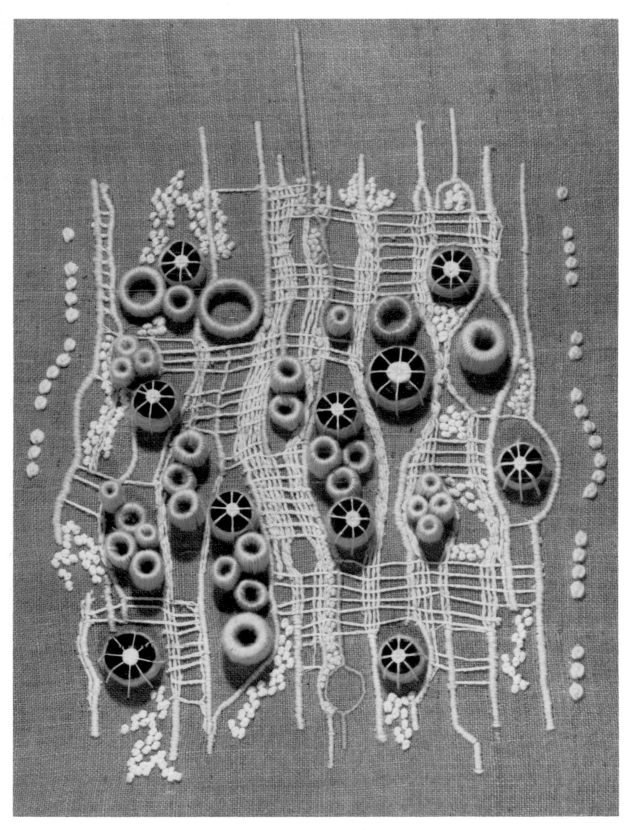

51 1970 – Audrey Tucker. *Campions.* **Hand embroidery on a cotton ground. Straight stitching using linen and flower threads and matt yarn**

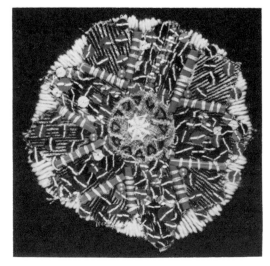

52 Right: 1969 – Bridget Pavitt, first in the Junior Section of the summer competition organised by the Embroiderers' Guild. A sea urchin on a turquoise and black fabric: '. . . . its main interest in the long red bugles couched down in white on applied striped fabric. The straight stitches in wool on the outer edge and the little beads and stitchery in the centre are beautifully done', *Embroidery,* **Volume XX, No. 4, Winter 1969**

The Seventies

The 1970s were years of indecision with political disasters and world recession. Although there was an appearance of stability at the beginning of the decade, this soon changed, with constant strikes because of trade unions demanding higher wages, increasing inflation, and prices doubling and trebling by the eighties.

The cinemas showed films which contained growing violence, as did television during the seventies. The so-called hippies became more settled, although their influence was maintained by an increased interest in health foods and those grown under natural conditions. This led to an awareness that conservation of the environment was necessary. Movements such as Women's Lib became less vociferous as the seventies advanced, although in the USA there were strong advocates for women's rights.

In retrospect, the decade was complicated politically, culturally and artistically, making it very difficult to obtain a clear view of things and therefore of the development of embroidery so near our own time. Attitudes and standards were changing and the craft developed along different lines. Small individual groups flourished, with new ones appearing during the decade.

Education

Many levels of embroidery were being promoted during the seventies. Professional embroiderers were teaching and executing commissions; amateurs were taking classes or working from the numerous patterns on the market or to be found in some women's magazines. Students were studying in selected colleges of art and polytechnics for the Diploma in Art and Design. Others in colleges of further education, where embroidery was a part of the courses, were able to study the craft as a creative medium and afterwards, as teachers, pursuing it in the schools. Embroidery was already a part of the art teaching programme, or there was a liaison between the domestic science, the needlework and the art departments, in a number of schools. The O and A levels school leaving examinations included embroidery in their curricula. Centres for the handicapped held classes for craftwork, including embroidery, while classes in adult education in arts and crafts flourished. As already mentioned, many women's magazines contained articles on a number of crafts concerned with fabrics and threads, among which were articles on embroidery for dress and for the home.

The Barry Summer School

A note on the Barry Summer School might be appropriate here, having been in existence from the beginning of the century with a long record of classes in a number of arts and crafts, including painting, photography, pottery, embroidery and weaving, also music and other arts and skills, conducted by many well-known artists as well as by embroiderers. The work was largely experimental and many people attended the School, often their first introduction to the craft being at Barry. Students needed no qualifications and could attend classes for one, two, three or four weeks, different tutors conducting each of the two-week courses. June Tiley has been a tutor of long-standing, conducting two weeks of the course each year.

The Diploma **The diploma colleges**

Nora Jones in an editorial comment in *Embroidery*, Volume 28, Number 3, Autumn 1977, on the 1970 diploma shows said that the four diploma colleges had already a vitality that was heartening and the evidence showed that 'embroidery is still firmly rooted in its highest traditions, but is being developed in terms of today'. Each of the schools with the diploma course had a different bias and approach to embroidery. Goldsmiths' School of Art had no fashion department so the trend was towards fine art.

In an interview that I gave in 1969, on the training of students for the Diploma in Art and Design, I pointed out that the students should realise that with a needle and thread as much or as little could be expressed, as with paint, clay or other media.

Both textile printing and weaving were a part of this course, as were these subjects in the other diploma colleges, thus giving scope for the making and decoration of fabrics, as well as their embellishment with embroidery. Birmingham, with a fashion area, produced some interesting embroidery for dress and accessories and, with weaving and textile departments, students were able to try out their ideas using mixed media. The department possessed too, a Schiffli machine which could produce multiple patterns with the pantograph method, thus, lengths of fabric could be embroidered with repetitive pattern suitable for industry.

In 1971, an account by **Joan Cleaver**, 'Embroidery, a Design Education', was on the training of embroidery students in the Department of Fashion and Textiles, City of Birmingham Polytechnic, where she was in charge of embroidery (19, 20). Among other points she said that embroidery had much to contribute to the education of a designer, the very complexity of the many techniques making it necessary to develop a sense of selectivity and refinement and an appreciation of the final purpose of what was being made. (*Embroidery*, Volume XXII, Number 1, Spring 1971.)

Loughborough possessed a fashion department so students could take advantage of this area of study as well as of printed and woven textiles. The training here was different in that students spent one year in general study, again with emphasis on drawing, specialising in embroidery and allied subjects during their second and third years.

Patricia Foulds (née Beese) wrote about embroidery at Loughborough College of Art and Design where she was in charge of embroidery. She said that each year the different thoughts and trends of students were stimulating; that she felt students were now more concerned with design than the medium, but were attempting to say something through it, and her aim was to avoid students being slaves to fashion. She thought that 'pop art' could have made people aware of the everyday objects around them and that, consequently, there was a less cold approach to design. (*Embroidery*, Volume XXII, Number 2, Summer 1971.)

Another account by **Anne Butler**, Head of embroidery in Manchester Polytechnic, Faculty of Art and Design, was written in 1970. In the article she said that the aim in studying embroidery in Manchester was to develop creative personal expression, although the future use of the subject was kept in mind; also that a student as a creative designer had to have the right attitude to exploring new materials, techniques and machines. (*Embroidery*, Volume XXI, Number 3, Autumn 1970.)

During the first term in the department students spent time in the four areas of textiles – fashion, print, weave and embroidery – making decisions for specialisation by the second term. Those students who chose embroidery, in their second year studied ecclesiastical embroidery as a part of the course. **Judy Barry** was the tutor for this subject which was compulsory.

These comments from artists in charge of embroidery in the four schools where students could study for the Diploma in Art and Design demonstrate the individual approaches of each to the subject, also the aims behind the curricula.

With the development of the degree course in embroidery the number of students training in the subject increased. The colleges of art and the polytechnics

1 1969 — Christine Risley. *Three Stars,* approximately 20 in. x 30 in. (51 cm x 76 cm).
The design grew from some moth-eaten patchwork round which the pattern was planned.
The red lines round the stars lead to red and orange tape outlines, with blocks of felt squares
and gold kid. Gold braid and plastic paillettes complete the idea
Photograph by Hawkley Studios

2 1966 — Elizabeth Geddes. *Night Owls.* Machine stitching on face cloth, with applied tweeds, wools and nets. Straight and satin stitch are used

3 1977 — Joy Clucas. *Fragmentation.* A panel using nets and transparent fabrics, with spots of solid colour and pleated and folded areas. Machine embroidery is used to carry out the work

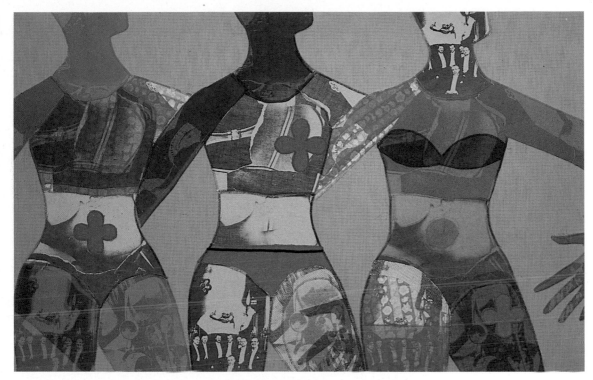

4 1969 — Maureen Helsdon. *The Three Graces,* 28 in. x 45 in. (71 cm x 114 cm). Selected photographs printed on a transparent silk organza, then cut and reassembled in layers, with appliqué added. Machine stitching on a bright green background

5 1971 — Maureen Helsdon. *Villa Garden.* A panel made for Royds' Board Room using photo-montage and applied fabrics on a dark turquoise ground with half-figures in dark and light skin colours. Pink and light navy with greyish mauve fabrics are applied

6 1969 — Eugenie Alexander. *The Owl in the Forest.* A panel, 20 in. x 21 in. (51 cm x 53 cm) using transparent fabrics *Photograph by Hawkley Studios*

7 1970 — Lilla Speir. *Burning Bush on a Summer Night.* A panel in silks, satins and velvets, partly padded, using dyes too, with hand embroidery

8 1974 — Beryl Dean. *The Temptation.* One of five panels completed in 1974 for St George's Chapel, Windsor. The embroidery, 9 ft x 4 ft 8 in. (2.74 m x 1.42 m), is worked on a handwoven linen lurex fabric, specially woven by Jack Peacock, with the colour graduated from light at the top to dark at the bottom of the panel. Techniques include gold work, drawn thread and pulled work, appliqué in fabrics and leather, with surface stitching

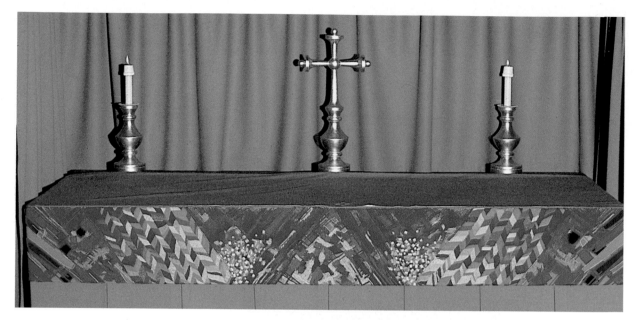

9 1975 — Judy Barry. A frontal in brilliant pinks, reds, greens and yellow-greens on a green background. Executed in machine stitching

10 1977 — Hannah Frew Paterson. Pulpit fall, 18 in. x 26 in. (46 cm x 66 cm), is based on the 23rd Psalm. It is in the Gorbals Church, Glasgow, a very modern building with a Burne Jones window beside the pulpit. The background colours represent passages from the Psalm: 'pastures green,' 'quiet waters' and 'death's dark vale.' The patched circle in silks, leathers and other fabrics, represents individuals. The three gold leather bands symbolise the Trinity. The structure is built up in relief from the background

11 1976 — Margaret Kaye. *Flowers*. A collage 9 in. x 7 in. (23 cm x 18 cm) in a variety of fabrics and colours

12 1970s — Kay Norris. *Persian Garden.*
A panel 11 in. x 9 in. (28 cm x
23 cm) carried out in gold threads with
the pattern in coloured silks worked over
the gold in the *or nué* technique
Photograph by Hawkley Studios

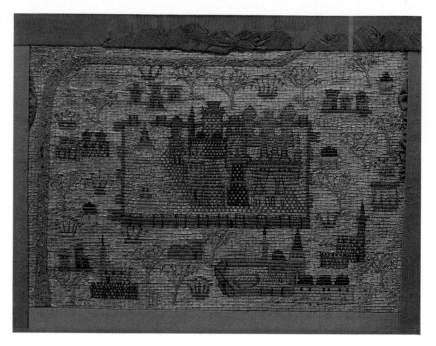

13 1977 — Kathleen Whyte. *Tree of
Light.* The panel, 33 in. x 38 in. (84 cm x
96.5 cm), depicts light shining through a
tree, the idea based on a painting
executed after a cataract operation when
the vision was somewhat distorted

continued to make their individual programmes, each with their particular trends. Manchester Polytechnic emphasised hand embroidery and industrial embroidery, Goldsmiths' School of Art tended increasingly towards fine art with less evidence of stitchery, Birmingham Polytechnic produced embroidery for dress, concentrating on this aspect perhaps more than did other colleges, while in Loughborough College of Art machine embroidery appeared to be favoured as well as constructions using fabrics and threads.

Later in the seventies, more comments on the degree shows were published. The Diploma in Art and Design became a BA honours degree qualification in 1975. At this time, too, Trent Polytechnic became a centre for the degree course in embroidery and textiles as a general study, whereas the other centres specialised in one main area with a subsidiary supporting one.

It was noted that in the Degree shows in 1976 the good work was supplemented by lively sketch books. **Margaret Nicholson** emphasised the importance of these in her article in *Embroidery*, Volume 27, Number 3, Autumn 1976, suggesting too that all students should keep sketch books on the commencement of their courses.

These shows became widely known and a considerable amount of experimental work was exhibited, using mixed media, often devoid of stitchery. People now were beginning to query work seen in the shows saying 'what is embroidery, where is it going? How will new graduates use their experiences?' Many queries were made on the survival of embroidery and the amount of techniques involved. There was concern that technique was insufficiently considered.

Nora Jones in her editorial comments (*Embroidery*, Volume 28, Number 3, Autumn 1977) said that a degree involved the training of the mind and that there was a long way to go to achieve full recognition of embroidery as a fine art, 'but there is also a danger that craftsmanship will be lost'.

Some of the students who had successfully completed their degree courses wrote articles for *Embroidery* on their approaches to their work. They described sources of ideas, how they resolved these into design and some of the problems that they had encountered. From these articles and the accompanying photographs, it appears that students were allowed to make their own decisions as to what types of embroidery they pursued.

City and Guilds examinations

At the Embroiderers' Guild in January 1970, an exhibition was held of work that had been submitted for the City and Guilds examinations. Notebooks, practical work carried out prior to the examination and examples of designs from the examination were displayed. This show gave some idea of work required and the scope of work entered for assessment.

In 1971 the Institute's examinations in embroidery were revised, several modifications being made, with new examinations starting in September 1971. A significant change was the introduction of the Common Core for domestic subjects, the title of which was now to be 'Home Economics and Creative Studies'. The embroidery syllabus was revised to 'suit the more mature student, as . . . a means of developing latent talent and to prepare them . . . for teaching and . . . other activities'. The examination remained in two parts, with the Common Core intended 'to . . . stimulate the students' critical faculties and arouse their interest in such topics as design and appraisal of materials'. In Part I also, the history of embroidery and machine embroidery were introduced '. . . with a broad interpretation, but . . . attention should be paid to contemporary trends in methods of work, colour and materials'. At both levels there was a written paper and a design paper with assessment of course work. See figures 104 and 114.

Adult education

Part-time students in adult education where the syllabus had been approved, were able to study over a set period for the City and Guilds of London Institute examinations in embroidery.

Classes such as those conducted at the Victoria and Albert Museum (see page 10), and others that commenced during the sixties, continued, thus spreading knowledge and increasing enthusiasm for embroidery.

Colleges of art continued to use mixed media – embroidery with knitting (71), dyeing and printing (70, 72) as well as with weaving, further combined with structures in wood, metal and plastics. Adult education classes were interested in embroidered boxes decorated in metal threads, beads and stitchery. Courses on embroidery in different parts of the country, exhibitions of work by both professional and amateur stitchers all helped to promote awareness of changes taking place in styles and techniques during the seventies.

Styles and ideas

The fashion for soft sculpture continued during the early seventies, with food (74, 118), objects and figurative ideas carried out in a variety of materials. Scale was an important factor, from full-sized figures to small dolls, from carrots 3 ft to 2 in long (90 cm to 5 cm). Food continued to be popular for design from giant size to miniature size, from the copying of reality as accurately as possible to almost abstract interpretations. A full scale soft refrigerator, filled with 'soft' food; 'soft' boxes; knitted and embroidered stuffed teapots and life-size human figures, were among the ideas seen during this time. Towards the end of the decade soft sculpture was less in evidence. Other ideas that were popular for some time were embroidered pictures of thatched cottages with country gardens of hollyhocks, lupins and other flowers, with clouds in the sky and often rainbows; these were also seen in other crafts such as jewellery, ceramics and printed textiles. Some of these subjects were culled from embroideries of the twenties, becoming characteristic images of the early seventies. Small, realistic landscapes (149), semi-abstract larger hangings based on landscape drawings, were often painted with dye and then embroidered. Geometric pattern combined with realism (jacket illustration), fabric manipulated as abstract form, pleated, gathered and folded, were continuing ideas.

Topical events, such as the moon landings, led to embroideries of the moon, images of outer space and the making of three-dimensional 'moon men'; portraits of well-known personalities such as film stars, pop idols and others were seen in canvas stitchery and collage. Abstract ideas continued too, with a simplification in the number of stitches employed in hand embroidery. This was noticeable in the work of students and professional stitchers as well as in that of amateurs. Machine embroidery began to dominate the scene in colleges of art with less hand stitching as the seventies advanced. Threads were dyed, embroidery was combined with frayed fabrics, stiffened fabrics, screen printing, fabrics of which the edges had been burnt or other devices used. Metal meshes were worked as in canvas using rug hooking techniques with fabrics cut on the bias, narrow ribbons, fine wire as well as yarns being employed in this way.

Patchwork became a craze towards the end of the decade (92, 123, 124), possibly inspired by the American bicentennial celebrations in 1976, when many stitchers became interested in quilt-making. In Great Britain the making of patchwork and quilted bedcovers and wall hangings have continued to attract attention.

Drawing by many amateur embroiderers was at one time considered by them as unnecessary, as their main interest was in technique rather than in design. This attitude was changing and in the late sixties a demand by those attempting to design for themselves was for classes and instruction in drawing. *Embroidery* magazine began to include articles on drawing leading to design, some articles being written by Audrey Tucker during the seventies. An article by Geoffrey Bailey in *Embroidery*, Volume 26, Number 2, Summer 1975, gave reasons for drawing. He said 'Designers using materials like fabric and thread feel an inbuilt commitment to the qualities and inherent characteristics of their materials and often find little real use for drawing'. He felt that 'drawing is perhaps the most economic and direct means of presenting a visual ideal. Part of the answer to defining something lies in the intention behind its purpose. What is important is that for a drawing to be such it must have a purpose . . . used within the context . . . as an important part of the designer's work they (drawings) are very much preparations. . . . They point towards opportunities for interpretation into whatever the designer wishes. . . . A drawing is an attempt to come to terms with a structural ordering'. He mentioned different ways of drawing and the intentions behind them. He concluded saying that 'Drawing lies at the root and stock of all areas of the visual arts'.

Embroiderers' Guild

The Embroiderers' Guild exhibition in 1972 at the Commonwealth Institute invited comments from different embroiderers on specific aspects of the craft and general comments by non-embroiderers on their impressions of the show. Among these Enid Jackson, for a time editor of *Embroidery*, thought that many wall decorations contained a superfluity of attached objects, while Colin Kirby Green, having criticised the '62 Group (page 13), said that his first impressions gave him nothing of note and that a better show would have resulted with half the number of exhibits. Among works of merit he selected Beryl Dean's patchwork frontal for Westminster Hospital, Audrey Walker's triptych *Out of Eden* (81), and Maria Theresa Fernandes' landscape as imaginative and original but that, with the amount of dye used, this could have been painted. He felt that Eirian Short's panel *Imortelle* possessed excellent technique, while Barbara Millie's red, very delicately worked circle was poorly presented, otherwise one of the most beautiful pieces of work in the show. Other embroiderers were mentioned, mainly showing landscape-inspired ideas. Nancy Kimmins exhibited a large canvas work *Rock Pool,* very dark and in relief, using coarse wools to make heavy textures.

Eirian Short was asked to 'write up' the exhibition . Doing this in a series of questions and answers she said 'Does the exhibition reflect current trends in art?', replying that with systems , progressions and mixed media and a breaking down of barriers in art, that some of the most successful panels in the show were in mixed media. She mentioned Audrey Walker's triptych (81) as being 'one of the most powerful pieces in the exhibition . . . its strength lies in the overall concept'.

She thought that the lack of vitality and style in the clothes was that they were 'safe and dated' and not of the present; also, too many pieces of work relied on technique and 'well worn themes'. Her answer to the work with a 'feeling of rightness' or that with 'an uncomfortable aura' was, she thought, due to the fact that 'those which are conceived from the beginning in terms of fabric and thread' felt right, but embroidery which 'could have been more suitably carried out in paint' was rarely satisfactory. Poor presentation was due to the lack of a total concept or to over elaboration. She compared the last exhibition at the Commonwealth Institute in 1966 with the present one, the most obvious change being in the use of mixed media, with knitting, crochet and macramé used in combination with stitchery. In spite of these criticisms the show was stimulating.

The Embroiderers' Guild exhibition, again at the Commonwealth Institute in October 1976, contained more panels and hangings than other exhibits. Quilts, boxes and dress embroidery were shown, but the comment on the latter was that 'many garments had been embroidered without enough consideration as to suitability of the style for decoration. It is important too, to think in terms of an entry which, although splendid when worn, will not necessarily display well in an art gallery'. (Editorial, *Embroidery*, Volume 28, Number 3, Autumn 1977.) Beryl Dean and Sylvia Green held a conversation about the exhibition, each expressing their views on what they felt. **Sylvia Green** thought that the show was more muted than the last one . . . that the embroiderer was now established with no need for flamboyancy. She did not approve of the movement towards 'so called soft sculpture' . . . and was interested in the comment of a sculptor who found the pieces 'unsatisfactory both as sculpture and as embroidery'. She also said that 'there must be a real reason for mixing techniques , several embroidery and other techniques were combined in the same work with success'. **Beryl Dean** thought that there was an emphasis on good draughtsmanship that was influencing embroidery. She found the Church work disappointing, but was pleased to see embroidered articles that were a part of everyday life, although some of the exhibits could only be kept in drawers, such as embroidered toys. She felt that the aim now was for ephemeral things for a limited use. She did not appreciate the chicken-wire structures, nor did the combination of paint and embroidery appeal to her, but she found the exhibition stimulating.

Another point of view in *Crafts*, January/February 1977, was that 'embroidery is alive and well'; Glenys Sida remarked on the fact that ten years ago 'machine embroidery was accepted, with some trepidation, into Guild exhibitions. Today this liberal approach has led to the acceptance of allied skills and textile forms such as tapestry-weaving, macramé, dyeing and printing, hand painted and sprayed fabrics, knitting and crochet'. The reviewer felt that besides extending the range of craft techniques, new aesthetic possibilities were offered, bringing the Guild into line with the teaching of embroidery as a degree subject. Her definition of craft as art was when the artist made decisions, not merely following set procedures and instructions. She found the successful sections in the exhibition within the areas of clothes, accessories and toys.

Exhibitions of historic embroideries always created interest, often promoting ideas for contemporary work and during July–August 1973 the Embroiderers' Guild put on an exhibition at the Victoria Art Gallery in Bath, 'One Thousand Years of Embroidery'. It received a record attendance.

The Young Embroiderers' Society

The Young Embroiderers' Society was launched in 1974, a great deal due to Lynette de Denne who also arranged the first exhibition of its work, held at Celanese House at the end of May 1974. There were four age groups and one of communal entries, all from schools. Work by older children was rather similar and showed a lack of personal feeling, but that of the younger children was less self-conscious in approach.

Competitions

In 1969 the Embroiderers' Guild had decided to hold a summer competition for embroidery by those under 18 years of age on 31 August 1969. There were two sections – one for those under 18, the other for those under 12 years of age. Three photograhs were provided as the basis on which ideas were to be based: a moth, a sea urchin and an onion seed head. The reason for the competition was to encourage boys and girls to enjoy making pictures in fabric, threads and beads. The results of the competition were individual, lively and of a generally high standard and so again, in the summer of 1970, a competition was set using photographs as before from which to gain ideas. The junior section in this competition produced good work, the senior section being less spontaneous.

The Challenge Cup competitions continued. Lynette de Denne commenting on the Members' competition in 1970 said that there was a wide variety of techniques shown in the work but 'the small number of rather mediocre entries' from the professional class suggested a lack of interest in the competition. In the amateur section there was a high standard of technical expertise but the work showed 'a lack of sparkle and originality'. (*Embroidery*, Volume XXI, Number 3, Autumn 1970.)

Again in 1971 the Challenge Cup competition for Members of the Guild was held, with some lively work entered in the amateur section. The professional section was disappointing with no award but in both sections, although they did not receive awards, there were some pieces of strong character. (*Embroidery*, Volume XXII, Number 3, Autumn 1971.)

In the Schools Challenge Cup competition for the same year, the senior cup was not awarded as the standard of work was not high enough, but the junior cup was awarded.

Experiment at Goldsmiths' School of Art

In the summer of 1970 an experiment was tried out. This was at Goldsmiths' School of Art. Students came from many parts of Great Britain, from the USA and other countries, to work on a collection of samples to be given to the Embroiderers' Guild for their portfolios. Each student designed her own pieces for specific techniques. These were worked out with the guidance of a specialist teacher. Three hundred samples were the result; fresh ideas and skills were experienced by the majority of the participants who made the samples and learned new ways of working at the same time.

Exhibitions

As a means of promoting embroidery and showing its versatility, as well as what could be accomplished with needle and thread, exhibitions continued to attract interest in the seventies. Both local and national shows were held during this decade by amateur and professional embroiderers but obviously cannot all be mentioned. Comments and descriptions of some of the shows, general trends and developments can be gleaned from individual viewpoints, from introductions to catalogues and from articles in magazines and newspapers. The Royal College of Art textile shows sometimes contained embroidery, the Diploma colleges (later, Degree colleges) held exhibitions of students' work as did other colleges of art; the London College of Fashion and colleges of higher education including colleges of education sometimes gave fashion shows containing embroidered garments, as well as displaying other embroideries, while exhibitions of examples of work by City and Guilds examination students were held. Groups held shows while some galleries accepted embroidery alone or as a part of mixed craft shows. Exhibitions of foreign embroideries also stimulated ideas.

A small gallery in London, Compendium 2, held a two-woman show in January 1970 of work by Anne Butler and Janet Graham, where each of them gave their views on their approach to work. **Anne Butler** said that she tried to keep in mind the factors relevant to pure embroidery, that materials and their qualities and her interpretation as two-dimensional compositions were important. The marks made by threads were related to weave/texture, surface/scale. Her examples were geometric, with limited stitches used to create textured shapes that enhanced the applied ones, often of fabric mounted over card. **Janet Graham** expressed her aim to keep work spontaneous with stitches used where needed for emphasis and to avoid the dominance of technique. She made quick notes from reality then worked away from these in order to avoid detailed clutter. She felt that designs for embroidery adapted to the materials used, but she based her ideas on memory, unconnected with a particular representational image. (*Embroidery*, Volume XXI, Number 3, Summer 1970.)

Commissions

Monarchy 1000, completed in 1973, was a commission for a wall hanging, to be placed in the Pump Room in Bath, to celebrate and commemorate the crowning of Edgar, the first king of all England, in Bath Abbey in the year AD 973. Audrey Walker designed and carried out the work (97). She found that she had a great deal of research to do on the historical aspect before she could start to design the panel, but was stimulated by the undertaking.

The Glasgow School of Art former students group of embroiderers held a show in the autumn where patchwork was popular. In fact, patchwork was creating interest now among stitchers, for household articles and dress accessories.

Glasgow Cathedral received a gift from Glasgow and the West of Scotland Branch of the Embroiderers' Guild. This was designed by Malcolm Lockhead and included a patchwork altar throwover with laid work and appliqué in gold and silver kid. See figure 95.

Another exhibition was shown at the Embroiderers' Guild headquarters in Wimpole Street, London, at the end of 1973. This was mounted by the Glasgow School of Art embroidery and weaving department and was the first time that they had exhibited there, also the first time that they had shown outside Scotland. H Jefferson Barnes, the Director of the School, paid tribute to Kathleen Whyte in his introduction to the catalogue, saying 'in an art school situation traditions can . . . be a hindrance rather than a help, and our particular debt of gratitude to Kathleen Whyte is that during the last 20 years or so she has taken these traditions, the techniques of the crafts, the old materials and a host of new ones, and has made embroidery and weaving as relevant an activity as any that are currently practised . . . the main purpose during all these years has been to inspire the creation of things to be enjoyed'.

The Crafts Council

Under the auspices of the Crafts Council, the Victoria and Albert Museum invited craftsmen in different disciplines to exhibit in the Museum in 1973. The exhibition was titled 'The Craftsman's Art' and included embroidery. Among those participating were Kenneth Dow Barker, Barbara Dawson, Christine Risley and myself. Christine Risley showed her *Three Stars* panel (colour plate 1) while I showed my double-sided banner *Night and Day*. Some of Kenneth Dow Barker's illustrations to *Stitch and Stone* were exhibited. See figures 43 and 44.

As this exhibition was successful the Director of the Museum, **Dr Roy Strong**, suggested that a small craft shop should be opened within the Museum. This materialised in August 1974. Textiles, pottery and jewellery were among the main categories of crafts for sale in the shop, also books and *Crafts* magazine.

Retrospective exhibition at Goldsmiths'

On my retirement as the Head of Textiles at Goldsmiths' School of Art in 1975, to mark this event a retrospective exhibition of 'Twenty-five Years of Embroidery' was arranged at the South London Art Gallery in June of that year. Early work appeared naive, designed and executed by non-art students; some pieces, too, showed a strong influence of my illustrative style during the mid-fifties. Other points were the use of fine black outlines slipped off the applied shapes, dating them as pre-1960. A noticeable tendency was the placing of designs centrally on fabric, almost like targets and isolated from the frames like vignettes. Later fifties' work was simplified and showed more abstraction, designs reached to the edges of frames, and unframed hangings were now appearing. Machine embroidery combined with hand, and larger pieces of work in appliqué, were in evidence at the end of the decade. Later examples showed a greater variety of ideas, mixed techniques and styles of work. Some students criticised the earlier work as static in comparison with that of the seventies. I would say that this was true and due to a lack of drawing by untrained, part-time students with little or no art background. Later examples showed more freedom in both drawing and design but with stitchery often an understatement.

Travelling exhibition

In Scotland a travelling exhibition was sponsored by Messrs J and P Coats and organised by the Scottish branches of the Embroiderers' Guild. This was called 'Embroidery in Action' and toured from the summer of 1975 through 1976 onwards. A varied selection of pieces included historic examples, work by school children and embroideries executed for Messrs Coats' publications. The theme was 'Design Through Embroidery'. Members of the branches exhibited their work simultaneously with the travelling show while it was in their district. By the enthusiasm shown, it was evident that there was a genuine interest in the craft.

The Royal School of Needlework

The Royal School of Needlework mounted an exhibition of historic and twentieth-century embroideries at the Royal College of Art for the Queen's Silver Jubilee in 1977. Lynette de Denne was asked to design and to display the work, which showed as its earliest piece of embroidery part of an orphrey on an English cope while the latest piece was one of the 34 panels of the *Overlord* embroidery (page 88). The embroideries came from many sources, including museums, private owners, the Embroiderers' Guild and the Royal School of Needlework itself. A great variety of exhibits was shown, some of historic value while others were displayed for their interest as embroideries. The Royal Household loaned a number of pieces of work.

Other exhibitions

Exhibitions by societies such as The Society of Designer Craftsmen, The New Embroidery Group, The Practical Study Group and others were held during the decade, in London and in the provinces. The Society of Designer Craftsmen, a group of craftsmen working in different disciplines, showed fewer embroideries than the others mentioned, which were embroidery orientated.

Throughout the seventies, branches of the Embroiderers' Guild held local exhibitions as well as those at Foyle's in London. The '62 Group held shows in London and in the provinces, the Contemporary Hangings exhibitions continued to inspire those who were unable to see the work of well-known embroiderers in the London galleries, and between 1966–76 there were seven Contemporary Hangings collections and three of Contemporary Pictures in Fabric and Thread. Besides these there were special collections of work to demonstrate methods and techniques. These included 'Creative Machine Embroidery', 'Embroidery – drawing, design and development', 'Macramé', and 'Embroidered Panels and Wall Hangings'. These collections were shown in many centres throughout Great Britain, in municipal galleries and colleges and made a great contribution in promoting textile crafts as well as in bringing to the public what was current in embroidery and other textile crafts.

Exhibitions by small groups were shown in churches, in libraries and in colleges of education. The diploma and, later, the degree students held annual displays of work in the colleges of art. An exhibition at the Whitworth Art Gallery in Manchester, 'The Turkoman of Iran', in mid-1972, was one with many ideas for the embroiderer, with its decorated hangings – often a collection of bits and pieces sewn together as squares and strips of fabric with rag fringing and sometimes feathers, buttons and odds and ends made into tassels. The embroidered costumes and the animal trappings, with their variety of cords and tassels, the richly coloured camel bags; all of these articles, of a nomadic race, were an inspiration to embroiderers who saw the show, as it travelled to other museums from Manchester.

In the foreword to a catalogue of embroideries shown at the Manchester Business School in 1973, it stated 'embroidery has now developed into a recognised art form . . . and . . . these artists embroider because it enables them to achieve textures and colours . . . not possible in any other medium . . . Embroiderers still employ the traditional techniques of stitching, quilting, padding . . . but . . . experimentation with new forms and techniques has led to a greater use of collage with embroidery'.

Among the exhibitors were Judy Barry, Anne Butler, Beryl Chapman, Ione Dorrington, myself, Moyra McNeill, Annwyn Nicholas and Herta Puls. The exhibition was arranged by **Anna Wilson** who had promoted much interest in embroidery in the area.

An exhibition by the Women's Institutes was held at the Commonwealth Institute in October 1975. This was pre-selected at county level first of all but the amount of work was so great that the display was somewhat overcrowded, making it difficult to see exhibits properly. In many cases the techniques were excellent with much of the work having a particular purpose, a commentator saying that 'one of the joys of the exhibition was the three-dimensional objects for many purposes'. Another commentator felt that the 'modern embroidery was not always of the high standard that one expected'.

In 1976 at the Commonwealth Institute, embroideries of the Hausa people of Africa were shown. These were collected by David Heathcote, an authority on the work, and were mainly examples of men's garments embroidered in brightly coloured silks or in monochrome. Designs were traditional, mainly geometric, worked in various stitches.

At this time, too, at the Crafts Centre of Great Britain, a collection of miniature textiles was shown, all 10 in. (25 cm) or less in size. A number of embroidered textiles were included.

Conservation

The conservation of textiles has become important during this century with both costume and embroidery now recognised for their historic and social significance; Karen Finch at the Conservation Centre at Hampton Court doing a splendid job of work. She had started a conservation studio in her own home in 1959. In the spring of 1975 the Conservation Centre was opened at Hampton Court after several years of hard work on the part of Donald King, Keeper of Textiles at the

Victoria and Albert Museum and the chairman of the advisory committee. The Centre works for museums, the National Trust and public and private bodies. The Courtauld Institute under the auspices of Karen Finch has a post-graduate course in textile conservation with the students working at Hampton Court in order to gain practical experience in the understanding of textiles.

As a conservationist Karen Finch has an international reputation, receiving the OBE in 1976 for her work in this field. Her aims are that textiles should be valued as 'historic documents', with the examples kept as near as possible in their original states and bearing in mind their situations when returned to their settings. The structures of fibres and cloths, the dyes and methods or work employed in the repair of embroideries, must be studied in order to counteract the deterioration. Wear and tear due to age and pollution of the atmosphere are also studied. Students have practical sessions too on different aspects of historic embroidery in order to understand some of the problems in conservation.

Kits

In the shops, many kits continued to be sold, such as reproductions of *The Laughing Cavalier*, French tapestries and woodland scenes, but also some kits that came from Sweden, contemporary in character, were scattered among the kits that had been seen in Great Britain for many years, some with patterns stamped on the canvas, others with charts to be followed. A gradual improvement in the design of some kits of British origin was seen although the old favourites continued to adorn the needlework shops and stores.

Magazines

The new magazine of the Crafts Advisory Committee, *Crafts*, was launched in March 1973, its aim 'to act as a bridge between the craftsman and his audience. It will also offer itself as a forum where craftsmen can debate issues of importance to them. It will keep track of technical developments in different fields and above all its aim will be to offer a service to the crafts'. (*Crafts*, March 1973.) Accounts of work of individual craftsmen and craftswomen, correspondence concerning these articles, often controversial, and information on trends, exhibitions and general crafts news were all part of the policy of the magazine.

Educational magazines entirely on needlework and allied subjects were being published too.

Ecclesiastical embroidery

Ecclesiastical embroidery during the seventies continued to be of interest to a number of artists with the Church giving commissions for vestments and furnishings. Exhibitions promoted these commissions too during the decade and in 1970 a special show of twentieth-century ecclesiastical hangings was presented at the King's Lynn Festival of Music, by artists connected with 'Contemporary Hangings'. Remarks on their aims were informative. **Richard Box** used religious themes with colour and texture to create atmosphere while **Anne Butler** was keen on pure stitchery and the marks made with threads, her main interest being the relationship between texture, surface and scale. **Joy Clucas** was concerned with colour and texture, using the Elements for design with such subjects as *Winter Cyclone*, *Dawn*, the *Sun and Moon*, and favouring circles and half circles for design in many of her embroideries. She said that she found the subject of Creation fascinating.

In November to January 1971–72 an exhibition of Victorian Church Art was staged at the Victoria and Albert Museum, London, with examples selected from different parts of the country and assembled with those from the Museum. This exhibition was the first of note on the subject with banners, frontals and vestments, mainly from the second half of the nineteenth century on view.

Group exhibitions continued during the year; the Embroiderers' Guild show at the Commonwealth Institute in 1972 was a highlight for both amateur and professional embroiderers. Different people were asked to give their comments on specific areas of work in the exhibition. Judith Scott, formerly the Secretary of the Council for the Care of Churches, now the Council for the Care of Places of Worship, commenting on the ecclesiastical embroidery, thought that there had been great advances in the last ten years with the invention of different techniques and the use of a great variety of fabrics. She felt that the purpose of ecclesiastical embroideries had been given insufficient thought, sometimes being too delicate for practicality, or decorated unsuitably with beads and sequins. Also she suggested that a fresh set of symbols could be designed for the present day, and that the embroidery should be designed to read from afar as well as close to. She felt, though, that the suitability of the article in question could only be judged in its setting.

One of **Beryl Dean**'s major commissions was completed early in 1974. This was a set of panels, started in 1970, for the Rutland Chantry, St George's Chapel, Windsor. She was asked to select five out of seven themes, choosing to begin with the Annunciation, which was followed by the Visitation, the Nativity, the Temptation (colour plate 8) and the Marriage of Cana. Fabric was specially woven for the embroideries by Jack Peacock. Drawn and pulled work, gold work, and appliqué in fabrics and leather were combined in these panels. When the embroideries were completed a retrospective exhibition was held in St Andrew's Church, Holborn, from April to May, of some of Beryl Dean's work including the panels, as well as that of her students. Fifteen years' work, from the first ecclesiastical classes at the Hammersmith College of Art and Building in 1958 up to 1974, was shown, embracing all aspects of embroidery for the Church. A group project, a stole, was presented to the Archbishop of Canterbury who opened the exhibition. In his introduction to the catalogue of the show, the Reverend Peter Delaney paid tribute to the work of a great British artist and craftsman, Beryl Dean. He said 'The exhibition shows not only Beryl Dean's own work but the work of her students and those she came in contact with. . . . A truly individual and characteristically English School of embroidery is well established, in fact a true inheritor of the great *Opus Anglicanum* period. It is largely due to Beryl Dean and her consistent love of her subject that people all over the world look to England for a lead in ecclesiastical embroidery'.

The Silver Jubilee cope (171), under the guidance of Beryl Dean, was completed in 1977, ready for the Jubilee celebrations. The design was to represent London and was conceived by Beryl Dean in 1975. As the embroidery was a communal effort she planned it in separate parts to be worked individually by members of her class. Her idea was to keep the overall effect delicate 'like a watercolour' as she said. The finished cope was presented to St Paul's Cathedral and worn for the Silver Jubilee service in June 1977.

In 1976, Hereford Cathedral held an exhibition of contemporary ecclesiastical embroideries, where again the well-known embroiderers of church work were represented. Among these were **Beryl Dean** with examples of work designed by her and carried out by herself and others, including some of her earlier examples – which had originally been commissioned by the Needlework Development Scheme and lent by the Victoria and Albert Museum. **Pat Russell** showed ten pieces, **Kathleen Whyte** exhibited a pulpit fall, as did **Hannah Frew Paterson** (150, colour plate 10), while **Barbara Dawson** showed three pieces. **Judy Barry** and **Beryl Patten** contributed many pieces while **Ione Dorrington** contributed a cope and a hanging and **Moyra McNeill** a stole and a kneeler.

Judy Barry writing on embroidery for the Church, said that there were 'practical considerations and restrictions when designing for the Church, as all things had particular functions and must be handled and cleaned. There were also restrictions on colours for the seasons of the Church year. The work (103) had to be kept within a budget, also different religions required different kinds of design and all these considerations must be understood before embarking on a design'. She stressed the point that the embroidery must unite with the architecture of the church, this involving scale and choice of colours to suit the surroundings as well as the purpose of the work.

Judy Barry and Beryl Patten took two years to design and make vestments including a cope and stoles and festal altar panels for Manchester Cathedral High Altar, starting in 1975 and completing them in 1977 (166). The aim of the designers was to make the altar attractive, also to reduce storage and handling to a minimum. They aimed, too, to reduce the appearance of the strong horizontal structure of the altar and the communion rail. Their plan was to design a Laudian frontal that could remain in place throughout the year but could be cleaned during Lent, solving the problem by designing detachable, free-hanging sets of embroidery in the appropriate liturgical colours of the Church seasons, which could be removed as required. (*Embroidery*, Volume 29, Number 4, Winter 1978.)

Materials

As time advanced, with cutbacks in industry and on imports of some materials, silk fabrics became less easy to obtain, Japanese gold threads disappeared and silk threads became scarce. Prices rose considerably, materials becoming very expensive by the 1980s, although this did not appear to deter the keen embroiderer. Silk threads were obtainable from France and Switzerland when unobtainable in Great Britain.

Dress

Clothes were sprayed or painted with dyes; patterns on these were worked in both hand and machine embroidery at the beginning of the seventies. Beading was seen on the more elaborate evening wear of well known designers.

Some students from Goldsmiths' School of Art were commissioned to design and embroider garments for *Vogue* magazine. Figures in the guise of dolls, clouds and rainbows were chosen as subjects with which to decorate these clothes, using dyes, painting, spraying, and printing, emphasising the patterns with hand and machine stitching and quilting. See figures 70, 71 and 72.

The layered look in clothes continued well into the seventies and there was no particular trendsetting; a certain drabness and dishevelled appearance with the wearing of a motley collection of garments of various lengths and patterns together, was noticeable among the apparel of the young. The ethnic look with the embroidered kaftans, the embroidered sheepskin coats from North Africa and Afghanistan, and garments from India and other eastern countries, all decorated with embroidery, became even more popular than in the late sixties. Jeans and tee-shirts with printed mottoes became almost uniforms. The 'junk' shops and the secondhand-clothes shops were searched for bargains, for garments to wear and for those that were suitable for cutting up for embroidery. Comfort and economy were more important than sophistication and elegance; the peasant look proliferated too.

A kind of nostalgia was noticeable with fashions of earlier decades returning, particularly those of the twenties, thirties and forties. In fact, things of the past became increasingly popular; old tunes, antiques and 1920s costume jewellery were now collectors' items. Even early plastic artifacts were being sought after, including dress ornaments.

Several dress designers at the beginning of the decade decorated their garments with embroidery: **Bill Gibb** placed swans, tigers' heads and other animals somewhat randomly on clothes, **Zandra Rhodes** used embroidery on some of her more extravagant creations while **Thea Porter** kept a shop filled with a collection of richly embroidered oriental costumes. The climate of the times encouraged the mixing of different styles and patterns of embroidery on one garment, with a tendency to the oriental, the kimono with its basically simple construction being introduced.

In 1970 an interesting scheme was carried out by **June Tiley** and **Diana Jones**, with students from the Cardiff College of Art and some from the Barry Summer School in Glamorgan, South Wales, where June Tiley was a tutor. Lord Bute launched a project for embroidered garments, to be designed and made from Bute Loom Tweeds, designed by **Martin Hardingham**. The collection was to be shown at the National Museum of Wales, fashions for day and evening wear to be presented with other types of garments and accessories. Plain and patterned tweeds were combined with a variety of fabrics including satin, velvet and leather. Canvas work, appliqué, smocking and patchwork were among the embroidery techniques employed. (*Embroidery*, Volume XXII, Number 1, Spring 1971.) (59 and 60.)

During the second half of the seventies there was an increasing interest in hand painting with dyes on silk, with patterns designed to suit individual garments and accessories. These patterns were often emphasised with embroidery and were quilted by hand or machine. Transfer dyes were used, too, to produce motifs on fabrics, further embellished with embroidery. **Zandra Rhodes** during this time was becoming known for her exotic clothes with her own patterns printed to complement the designs. Originally a textile designer, she used her fabrics exclusively for her printed garments, adding hand embroidery to emphasise edges and areas of print. **Sue Rangeley** was also becoming known for her painted garments and accessories, hand embroidered and quilted and later machine embroidered. Fabrics were often dyed in subtle colours and made into patchwork garments, with plain and patterned pieces used together. Styles were sometimes based on ethnic costume and vivid coloured fabrics, lace, ribbons, embroidery and beads were intermingled for elaborate creations. The kimono with its simple shape became popular as a basis for hand stitched pattern or quilted pattern by hand or machine.

Towards the end of the seventies machine stitched cut work decorated garments in the better boutiques. Blouses, skirts and accessories in fine fabrics were fashionable, sometimes with only parts decorated, sometimes a complete garment had an all over cut-work pattern, made from yardage. Smocking became another means of decorating adult clothes, sometimes freely worked and assymetrical in style, with fabric gathered at random and usually in fine chiffons, silks or lawn.

Theatrical costume

Embroidery for costume plays on television was a field of work that was expanding continually, considerable historic research being necessary for accuracy of detail. A notable serial film, one based on the life of Henry VIII, contained costumes with simulated embroidery using nuts and bolts, tap washers, buttons, cords and bits and pieces; nothing to do with real embroidery but embellishment that was effective in its large scale treatment of decoration. 'In *Elizabeth R*, a later historical film, the Elizabethan costume was embellished with machine embroidery, but to give the appearance of handwork. The elaborate use of beads, sequins and pearls with embroidery worked on the Irish and Cornely trade machines, however, still took much time to accomplish. Information on the stitchery was gathered from the exhibition 'The Elizabethan Image' at the Tate Gallery in London (1970) and from portraits of the period elsewhere. Much of the embroidery was worked freely with all-over pattern to give a richness to cheap fabrics while other stitching was precise and carefully copied from the paintings. The embroidery was carried out by Phyllis Thorold OBE and Georgina Wilsher.' (*Embroidery*, Volume XXI, Number 4, Autumn 1971.)

The '62 Group

This group formed during the sixties continued to flourish, while others were formed during the seventies. It held a number of exhibitions in London and in the provinces and invited different artists to comment on the shows, these comments being recorded in *Embroidery*. Criticisms of some of the shows appeared in other publications too.

Colin Kirby Green, a painter, commenting on the exhibition by the '62 Group at Congress House in June 1970 said that 'the exploitation of new and attractive materials for their own sake is, in all the arts, a worn out activity'. He remarked, too, on clichés of previous years and the 'pretentious work of many of today's contributors' but concluded that the exhibition was an improvement on those of the two previous years. (*Embroidery*, Volume XXI, Number 3, Autumn 1970.)

The '62 Group continued to hold exhibitions each year. In 1971, at Congress House, the work was more figurative than abstract. **Eirian Short** contributed *Swans in Love*, **Dorothy Reglar**'s work was mainly in beads while **Jennifer Gray** showed her experiments exploring light on fabrics and the use of 'shot' fabrics (33). Individual characteristics were noticeable. **Alison Barrell** showed *Green Dorset* (74), one of series of landscapes in monotone, while **Beryl Chapman**'s work was again geometric in style. **Audrey Walker** contributed her largest piece of embroidery so far – *Pool in the Garden* (82) developed from drawings made in Portugal. The Group for the first time showed work outside London, too, at the National Museum of Wales in Cardiff.

The '62 Group in their catalogue in 1972 emphasised their aims which were 'to exhibit new work rather than established embroidery, to as many people as possible; to improve the image of embroidery and to increase the standard in schools by making it an exciting subject; to work closely with industry in improving industrial embroidery by interesting manufacturers in freelance design;

to further the interests shown by the public in articles and books on embroidery by bringing the talents of the Group to the notice of the publishers; to improve communication through discussion of work'.

In 1972 to mark the tenth anniversary of the Group, a show was held where all exhibits were to be 10 in. (25 cm) square. This was held at Congress House in London. **Jan Beaney** commented that out of the 72 exhibits only five or six were 'very exciting', as although there was variation in the work there was a lack of vitality with the small sizes of the entries in danger of being over cluttered. Stretching a point, several works showed multiples of the square, one of these by **Alison Barrell** who said that 'a great deal of embroidery today contains "exciting new" threads, used in "exciting new" stitchery on exciting, often textural fabrics and the result seems to me to be too much of a good thing'. She felt that the set discipline of the exhibition was a good experience and that it should stretch one's versatility. **Richard Box** talking of his own work found that the effect of a square to him was static, cold and unmoving; he found that a rectangle had enough variation in its proportions to make the shape more interesting, but that the square was a challenge, the size stipulated attracting him by its smallness. He presented squares in various fabrics including leather, suede and thread in a series of small pictures of the *Orpheus and Euridice* legend. **Maria Theresa Fernandes** used various techniques in a free approach, saying that generally she worked on a large scale but recently had been experimenting with smaller panels based on drawings of landscape. She said that the panels were sketch-like, quick, spontaneous marks made on fabric rather than on paper. To her, embroidery was a fine art and working on a small scale had helped her in exploiting more techniques and in keeping the spontaneity of the subject, not always possible on a large scale.

In 1974 the '62 Group launched its most ambitious exhibition, 'Embroidery at Work', at the Commonwealth Institute in London. It was also the largest with the work of each exhibitor hung as a group, including drawings and sketch books. Weaving was shown for the first time, examples being embellished with embroidery. Among comments it was said that '**Heather Padfield**'s drawings were deceptively simple while those of **Audrey Tucker** were complex but with selective detail, her embroidery of landscape following the drawings quite closely'. (133, 134) **Irene Ord** showed geometric design, **Anne Butler** a quilt with a minimum of stitching, **Dorothy Reglar** two large panels of trees in fine fabrics (107), while **Moyra McNeill**'s footstool decorated with embroidered feet was, I thought, a witty contribution. **Eirian Short** writing on her *Death* panels (79) said that 'thoughts of my work are with me . . . through most of my waking day. Working with this sort of commitment in embroidery or collage or any other medium, is far removed from the treatment of these media as pastimes, to be picked up when time allows. The work is not done for the pleasure of doing it but because it is the best way of achieving the desired result'. She found that concentration on one subject had the advantages of studying in depth rather than flitting from one theme to another and felt that 'The mind should be constantly on the alert and open to stimuli from wherever they may come . . . and if a piece of work is more interesting for the way it is done than for what it is trying to say, there is to my mind, something wrong'. (*Embroidery*, Volume 25, Number 3, Autumn 1974.)

Another view on this '62 Group show said that the clearest expression was in examples of three-dimensional work, two of Alison Barrell's embroideries being mentioned, *Roller Coasters* and *Country Seat*. The reviewer, Michael Regan in *Crafts* magazine September/October 1974, mentioned nature as still a favourite theme but only successful when handled in a three-dimensional way. He concluded that basically the exhibition re-affirmed the aims of the Group saying that 'with exhibitions of this type, embroidery may revive its status as a valid and fully creative medium'.

In the summer of 1975 the '62 Group again held their exhibition at Congress House, this time of 'stabiles' or free standing objects. Denys Short wrote a review of the show saying that 'my primary interest is in ideas and whether they are effectively expressed. No medium is inherently more satisfactory than another in enabling the artist to express himself; each has its own good qualities, problems and limitations'. He felt that space had not been used as it could have been, in the works shown, although there was variety of outlook. Among works mentioned he thought **Heather Clarke**'s *Vase of Flowers* (88) and **Alison Barrell**'s landscapes were successful (127).

In June 1977 the '62 Group exhibition at Congress House was reviewed by David Green, a senior lecturer in printed textiles at Goldsmiths' School of Art. His comments were recorded in the autumn number of *Embroidery* in 1977. He quoted their statement that '. . . the '62 Group is concerned to promote high professional standards and to provide opportunities for exhibitions of work by young, newly qualified embroiderers. He said that 'the statement may have been true when embroidery was taken out from the yoke under which it had laboured, as being simply "one of the crafts". . . . I fear that it is no longer able to consider itself as reflecting fully the major change taking place throughout the embroidery-textile field. There are familiar names but the exhibition although well and professionally presented . . . in general is middle of the road and safe'. The show was small, so emphasised the lack of change in the group. David Green queried the craft of embroidery as an art form and said that the exhibition was restating much that had been going on in embroidery for a long time. He implied that the '62 Group was needed, but that it had to be strong and needed the membership of those who might be pushing embroidery further and wider.

Ann Sutton reviewed this exhibition too, remarking that 'embroidery' was the new dirty word of 1977 and that it was omitted from the poster advertising the show, this being entitled 'Textile panels, hangings and soft sculpture'. She felt that prices were unrealistically low but was pleased to find that the catalogue was related to the sequence in hanging. Several works that she mentioned were Rosalind Floyd's *Window Box*, Eirian Short's *Kosy Cottage*, nostalgic with 'a magical ambiguity of materials' while Audrey Walker's tentative, drifting image worked. Disappointments were Julia Caprara's work which was more careless, while she felt that Verina Warren was beginning to churn work out. (*Crafts* September/October 1977.)

Some exhibitors and members of the '62 Group were upset by David Green's criticism of the show. Audrey Walker, the president, replied saying that she disagreed with some of his statements among which he said that only one aspect of embroidery was shown. She disagreed, too, with his view that work over three years old should not be considered and pointed out that the selection panel changed annually but did not receive for selection the 'uncomfortable, controversial work that he felt was necessary'. In her conclusion she wondered if artists could afford to show 'really experimental work that won't sell'. She said 'have we come to a plateau . . . with a few artists with a strong enough personal vision to lift embroidery . . . into the area of enduring art?'. (*Embroidery*, Volume 28, Number 4, Winter 1977.)

The '62 Group exhibited at the Greenwich Theatre Gallery in December 1977. Framed panels only were allowed owing to fire regulations. Irene Ord said that in hanging the show, size, shape, colour and texture were more important than subject matter. Landscape was most popular; gardens, parks, buildings and a few geometric panels were also seen. Some styles were abstract, others realistic. The trend was to fine stitchery rather than bold. She wondered how the '62 Group would resolve the dual role of artist-craftsman in the future.

Other groups

The Practical Study Group was originally Group '73, but is now known under its present title. Among its founders were **Daphne Nicholson** and **Diana Keay** who had taken the combined course at Loughborough College of Art and Design and at the University of Nottingham, Department of Adult Education. There they had obtained the certificate of the Leicestershire Education Committee. The aim of the Group was to further interest in design and embroidery through adult teaching in any part of the country other than in London. The Group expanded but candidates had to show work for selection, and after five years were re-assessed for continued membership. A number of people had taken the Loughborough course before becoming members. As the work of the Group developed and those teaching became known, exhibitions were planned, taking place in different centres.

Another centre that promoted an interest in embroidery and other crafts was sponsored by the Leicestershire Education Department. This was a resource centre for design at Loughborough College of Art and Design which had been previously for Leicestershire teachers only and was now open to anyone. It had facilities for various crafts in the studio workshop, a common room, sources of art and craft supplies, with specialist tutors who gave advice when required on aspects of crafts. It was hoped that the Centre would fill a need for teachers who missed the stimulation of a college and wished to continue their own work.

Craft workshops

The Beckenham and Penge Adult Education Centre and Textile Studio

In 1970, the Textile Studio at the Beckenham and Penge Adult Education Centre came into being, its history going back to the sixties when the Beckenham and Bromley schools of art were amalgamated as the Ravensbourne College of Art. When **Iris Hills** left Bromley College of Art in 1955 (see *Twentieth-Century Embroidery 1940 to 1963*, page 51), **Freda Coleborn** took over the embroidery department but, sadly, she died in 1964. **Margaret Forbes** then organised it but owing to the lack of space in the new college, the embroidery was transferred to the Adult Centre in Beckenham in 1967 where the classes expanded rapidly. Margaret Forbes, tutor in charge at this time, pointed out that with mixed abilities these classes were too large so, at her suggestion, a group that could work on its own and carry out experimental projects was formed. This group was composed of ten students with **Alison Barrell** in charge to advise, but not to teach, as these students were professional or semi-professional artists who wished to work together and to exchange ideas and expertise.

Alison Barrell became Tutor in Charge of the Textile Studio in 1970. This flourished with her encouragement and experimental attitude, which gave the students freedom to do what they wished and to work in a more personal manner without tuition. Landscape and figurative themes were favourite subjects, with drawing an important adjunct. Facilities for drawing, for suggestions on techniques and on the history of embroidery were there for anyone who required them as the adult centre trained students for the City and Guilds examinations in embroidery under the tutelage of **Moyra McNeill**, with **Barbara Siedlecka** teaching drawing and **Nancy Kimmins** history of embroidery. Discussions on the craft, with shows held frequently, including a major exhibition each year, have kept the workshop flourishing.

The Studio was commissioned to make an embroidery for the entrance to the Embroiderers' Guild stand at the Ideal Home Exhibition held in March 1973. The theme of house and garden was designed in sections as a group project taking four weeks to carry out, under the instructions of Barbara Siedlecka and Alison Barrell. Mixed techniques included knitting and crochet, large pompons, fabric stretched over polyester foam and card. The result was of bold high relief (98). (*Embroidery*, Volume XXIV, Number 1, Spring 1973.)

The Weatherall Workshop

In Coleford near the Forest of Dean, the Weatherall Workshop was opened in 1973, with **Lillian Delevoryas** one of its residents. She was well known for her canvas embroideries, was also a painter, and produced wall hangings, cushions and embroidery for chairs as well as appliqué on garments. Most of her colour was subtle and many commissions were received. **Robin Ames**, a wood-turner who administered the Workshop, was also a resident together with two trainees. **Kaffe Fassett** and **Richard Wormersley**, both workers on canvas, were part of the group, which received a grant from the Crafts Advisory Committee about 18 months after its opening in order to help to increase the workshop area. Weekend courses were held and exhibitions mounted, attracting a number of visitors. The Workshop no longer exists.

An idea by **Michael Haynes** to provide working spaces for artists and craftsmen to work in groups, came to fruition in 1970 with the opening of the complex of studios called $401\frac{1}{2}$, in London, where several now well-known textile artists started their careers. Among these were **Diana Harrison** and **Philippa Bergson**, both of whom studied embroidery and had been on post-diploma courses at the Royal College of Art. The studios were successful, allowing the young artists to work on their own, but not in isolation, to work without expenses being too heavy, so to obtain a start that without the work spaces might have been difficult.

In 1975 Michael Haynes was offered a manor house in the Cotswolds, known as Fosseway House, where a group of young artists set up workshops. Among these was **Sue Rangeley** who was becoming known for her painted, dyed and embroidered clothing and accessories (page 83).

Craft societies The Red Rose Guild

The Red Rose Guild during the period 1963–74 held a permanent exhibition in South King Street, Manchester, staged by the Northern Crafts Centre Ltd, a limited company registered as a charitable institution sponsored by the Red Rose Guild. This Centre closed in 1974 at the end of the lease on the premises. The Guild had an exhibition in 1971 at the Whitworth Art Gallery to celebrate its fiftieth anniversary. From that date until 1976 the Guild remained inactive, but through a lay member, Dr Henry Spittle, the Whitworth Art Gallery put on another successful exhibition.

The Federation of British Crafts

The Federation of British Crafts was formed in 1970, its aim 'that all crafts should be represented by a single body', and that each craft society should choose a representative to attend meetings on behalf of that society. The Embroiderers' Guild became a member as did many craft guilds and societies who hoped to keep in touch with current happenings through the Federation.

In the autumn of 1971 the Crafts Advisory Committee was formed, its aim to promote British artist craftsmen, helping to maintain and improve their work and bring it to the public to show what was being done as well as to encourage sales. Various grants, loans and bursaries were forthcoming while the Government grant to the crafts was administered by the Committee in ways most beneficial to craftsmen. Among those receiving grants and loans there were several embroiderers in the early years of the Committee's existence and others during the decade. The Embroiderers' Guild received a grant towards the 1972 exhibition at the Commonwealth Institute.

In May 1972, after long and arduous discussions, the Crafts Centre and the Crafts Council combined as the British Crafts Centre, which was open for membership to anyone interested in the crafts, as well as those wishing to exhibit work.

In 1973 the Crafts Advisory Committee bought the gallery in Waterloo Place, while the British Crafts Centre retained the Earlham Street premises.

Community projects

Many community projects were started at this time, among these were schemes for Chester, Newcastle, Bedford, Northampton and Greenwich, to name a few. The Jubilee cope (171) for the Queen's Silver Jubilee was another example as was that later on, carried out for Maidenhead. These community efforts were often planned by one artist who also co-ordinated the work. The design was arranged in such a way that a number of people were able to embroider individual pieces, the completed work being assembled at the end into a series of panels or one larger embroidery.

Some of these group projects can be mentioned briefly. The Canterbury hanging (105) was designed by **Elizabeth Hammond** and worked by the East Kent Branch of the Embroiderers' Guild. Another project worked by the same group and designed by **Ruth Issett**, was a quilt based on the environment in East Kent. Flowers, fields and cliffs were applied in a variety of fabrics and colours. Having taken just over a year to make, the quilt was finished in 1976. The Northamptonshire screen, designed by **Pauline Allett** had similar designs on both sides, but colours were varied, one worked in those associated with spring, the other in those associated with autumn.

The *Overlord* embroidery which was begun in 1969 was finished in 1974 but was seen for the first time by the public at Whitbread's Brewery in Chiswell Street, London, in 1978. Lord Dulverton commissioned the embroidery as a tribute to the allied forces in the Second World War. The complete work consists of 34 panels. It was designed by **Sandra Lawrence** with advice from three senior officers of the Armed Forces, and the embroidery was executed in appliqué with 20 embroiderers working on it for five years at the Royal School of Needlework.

The *Chester Tapestry* so called, although in reality canvas work, was conceived in 1975 to mark the European Architectural Year. The finished embroidery, to hang in the Town Hall, was sponsored by the Chester Arts and Recreation Trust. The design by **Diana Springall**, has as its theme 'Chester Today' and is based on the surrounding pastoral scenes. Ten main panels and four frieze panels make up the complete design which includes buildings in Chester and Friesian cows, the source of the famous Cheshire cheese.

Embroiders in the Seventies

Alison Barrell found beads and *objets trouvés* fascinating. She experimented with traditional techniques such as blackwork and pulled-thread work. From these her interest in padding developed and during the early seventies she was producing a number of padded landscapes in which she incorporated covered cardboard tubes, or card covered with fabric and thread. *Green Dorset* (74) is an example of padded relief embroidery. *Red Dorset*, another version, was worked in a similar manner, from the same subject. See figures 55, 74, 93 and 127.

Judy Barry and **Beryl Patten** have worked together on commissions since 1973, mainly for ecclesiastical interiors. They use machine stitching and appliqué in executing the designs, their ideas evolving jointly through discussion, which are a fusion of both their styles into one. They have found that working together is stimulating. The designs are on a scale to suit the buildings for which the work is intended, each commission posing certain limitations, a challenge in itself. Consideration is given to the use of symbolism, liturgical colours and the purpose of the work within its setting as well as to its practicality.

They have found it necessary for economic reasons to use machine embroidery, but find too, that for them, the technique has as much or more versatility than hand work. Copes, chasubles, altar frontals, dossals and smaller items of church furnishings are tackled in their partnership of 'Embroideries for Interiors'. They carry out many commissions, a large number of which are for places of worship – churches, synagogues, and others – involving particular disciplines. See figures 103, 166 and colour plate 9.

Since 1974 **Jan Beaney** has produced mainly wall panels of landscapes, seascapes and atmospheric effects based on changes in the weather. She finds the possibilities of the different surfaces of fabrics chosen to express ideas, coupled with the textures of threads, intriguing. Appliqué with hand and machine stitching, on the domestic machine, with padded areas and raised stitches as well as the contrasting of textured fabrics, give her work its particular character. She finds that her choice of colours can also express many of her ideas, using subtle tones or brilliant ones and strong contrasts.

Anne Butler during the sixties was a lecturer on embroidery at Goldsmiths' School of Art, at the end of the decade taking charge of embroidery at Manchester Polytechnic where she became principal lecturer.

Her work is geometric in style, with mixed techniques, employing appliqué, padding, fabric stretched over card, canvas work and surface stitchery, mainly by hand. She uses a limited number of stitches in each example, to express different ideas, changing their scale and spacing, also the direction of working in order to obtain subtle variations of tone and texture. Some fabrics are manipulated by tucking and pleating with machine tufting.

Her ideas are planned with care, nothing is haphazard; economy of line, form and colour to say what she intends are characteristic features of her work. She can change scale from quite small examples to large hangings if required. See figures 75, 76 and 102.

Julia Caprara teaches both children and adults, finding inspiration and impetus for creative thinking from this work. She likes contrasts in textiles such as soft and hard, shiny and matt, warm with cool colour, so finds textiles a constant stimulus. The content of her work develops from a struggle and search to relate objective imagery and the natural/man-made world and in opening up symbolic and fantasy areas of the unconscious. Sometimes poetry gives her the title of an image, sometimes a word will begin and evolve round a found object or a fragment of fabric or a texture. She rarely draws but builds up ideas as she proceeds.

Joy Clucas specialises in machine embroidery although using hand stitching occasionally to emphasise details. She shows skill in her fine line work, covering large areas of fabric in straight stitching, sometimes incorporating appliqué in transparent or opaque fabrics. Some of her designs merge from one colour to another, such subjects as sunsets, sunbursts, celestial forms and abstract patterns having an appearance of depth with the variation in the spacing of the lines of stitching. The closeness or openness of these lines created tonal values. See colour plate 3.

Ione Dorrington became interested in ecclesiastical embroidery and recently concentrated on this work, carrying out designs for a number of copes and chasubles, as well as altar frontals. She also experimented with free-hanging, non-rectangular, three-dimensional forms, that sometimes are in mixed media and employ a variety of fabrics. Some of her ideas have been developed from the brilliant Thai silks that she possessed, others from drawings of everyday objects, while some designs are geometric. Much of her work is executed in blind appliqué with embroidery in silk and metal threads, limited in amount. Her colours are brilliant, often applied to white silk backgrounds.

Joyce Conwy Evans in 1975 started her own practice and has designed a number of textiles that include embroidery. She has also designed woven hangings, executed by the Edinburgh Tapestry Company and other embroideries carried out by **Elizabeth Geddes** (34). Her designs are theatrical, heavily decorated, often jewelled. She plans everything carefully on paper in order to obtain the effect that she hopes to achieve, working usually to scale as she designs for large pieces of work.

Patricia Foulds endeavoured at Loughborough College of Art and Design to give students a sound technical knowledge of both hand and machine embroidery, while at the same time trying to develop their individual creative potential. She is interested in fairgrounds and their wealth of patterns, in fragmentation and the breaking down of forms into small, lively areas that are rebuilt into new patterns. She carries out both secular and ecclesiastical embroidery.

Diana Harrison worked at the studios of $401\frac{1}{2}$ for some time, among other things, designing fabrics for Michael Haynes, the instigator of the studios. She was trained as an embroiderer and uses machine quilting for most of her hangings which are abstract in pattern, often geometric and printed, spray dyed or splatter dyed in near tones of subtle colours. The quilting is varied in depth and density, so changing the quality of surface textures, all the designs being planned carefully and executed with precision. She uses synthetic rayon satin (acetate) for her work with disperse dyes, and besides hangings produces quilts and cushions.

Maureen Helsdon continued to teach and to exhibit. In 1970 she showed work at the Alwin Gallery which usually showed fine art. From this exhibition a number of commissions followed, including one for Royds advertising agency (colour plate 5), which was for a series of panels for the Board Room. She uses photo-montage, screen printing and embroidery, maintaining her interest in the human figure (129), although she designs also from all kinds of natural form, usually working in machine stitching. See colour plate 4.

Polly Hope, originally a painter, carries out large three-dimensional hangings which she calls 'stuffed pictures', often with wit and with life-sized figurative subjects. She also designs and carries out fantastic clothing such as dresses covered in trailing foliage, stuffed birds and flowers with silk and metal thread embroidery, or garments with unicorns and fabulous beasts, applied and enhanced with many sequins and beads. She exhibits in a number of galleries, including those in London and New York. For a part of the year she lives in Lindos on Rhodes where quilt making is a specialist local craft, so she employs a veteran quilt maker, named Adonis, to assist her. She made her first examples in 1976 and collects fabrics everywhere, using plain-coloured backgrounds, sometimes applying six or more layers of fabric, stuffing and stitching them, elaborating these three-dimensional panels with beads, sequins and embroidery. See figures 163 and 164.

Diana Jones, through becoming interested in canvas work with the limitations of the grid and of geometric pattern (83, 152), began to think about patchwork. She pieced fabrics, building them up using pleated and interwoven strips. At present her concept is that function can also become decoration, which she says fascinates her.

In 1974 **Joan Marsh Jones** was granted the first Churchill Fellowship in embroidery to do research in Turkey, on Turkish embroidery and on symbolism in ancient civilisations.

Janet Ledsham works from her environment; in the summer interpreting the landscape of Northern Ireland, on the spot, into embroidery using straight stitching for spontaneity; in the winter she works from her own photographs and colour slides for her designs. She has been influenced by her training as a painter, working sometimes in broad areas of colour, with stitch textures in hand embroidery.

Lesley Miller stayed in Orkney for a time and was influenced by the Swedish folk traditions and textile crafts, leading to her more pictorial style of work some of which is executed entirely in chain stitch. She likes strong, brilliant colour, using different textures of yarn and unspun wool laid on rough surfaces to give raised effects; her ideas are often based on landscape and rock forms.

Alison Liley, now living in Ireland, is creating patchwork articles, and producing knitting and screen printing, saying that as a teacher she feels that she acted as a catalyst in promoting students' interest but also in giving them confidence in developing their own ideas.

In the mid-seventies, **Joan Nicholson** designed some canvas packs that allowed individual initiative, filling a gap for those who feel that they cannot design, also encouraging young people to see what they can do with colour and stitch (153). Her designs for greeting cards have raised the standard of canvas work above the usual level of commercial patterns. For Messrs J and P Coats she has designed square or circular shapes, about $3\frac{1}{2}$ in. to 3 in. (9 cm to 7.5 cm), in attractive folders, of butterflies, flags and geometric patterns in basic colours. Some of the squares have been designed as square cushion covers, but the small shapes are intended as patches to be sewn together in any way required. She has also designed canvas ideas for *Golden Hands* magazine, such as waistcoats, small bags and accessories, all depending on an individual arrangement of the motifs.

Irene Ord has been using the square as a basis of design since 1973. She has found that fabrics and threads are the best means of developing her ideas for non-functional design. She has worked on systems, grids, overlapping grids and repetition of a unit, making a basic statement on paper which she gradually enriches and expands as the idea unfolds. Both fabrics and threads and ideas integrate to form complicated pattern. She uses hand and machine stitchery according to what she wishes to express, also chooses colours, often dyeing her fabrics, to give subtle or bold effects.

Jane Page has continued to teach children from junior to senior level (125, 126), her aim in teaching embroidery in schools to develop the children's awareness by observation and by handling fabrics and threads to begin to understand their potential, with technical knowledge being discovered as the need arises. She is still interested in designing intricate pieces of work using traditional techniques such as pulled work, darning and other counted-thread methods based on the types of materials used. Often she combines several of these in one piece of work.

Hanna Frew Paterson carried out work for interiors but concentrated on church commissions for pulpit falls (150, colour plate 10) and other works where three-dimensional structures could be explored. She says 'I have always been interested in the three-dimensional aspect of threads and materials producing textural effects with stitchery. I am also keen on the possibilities of metal thread embroidery'.

Herta Puls, who has visited the San Blas Islands several times, has become interested in the work of the San Blas Indians and their molas, with the consequent writing of her book on 'cut work' with special reference to the techniques employed in the making of the molas. She has carried out her own work using their method of working and has also executed panels in appliqué, often padded. She has produced small structures in threads that appear to change in colour according to the angle from which they are seen. She is keen to see the use of fabrics and threads and embroidery in schools as a part of general education, where, linked to other subjects, it could be a stimulus to invention. See figure 99.

As a student **Sue Rangeley** was not interested in colour. She painted in black and white. However, she was always interested in textiles and in 1975 gave up teaching to concentrate on embroidery. Her interest in appliqué and quilting developed; her designs for cushion covers, small bags and dress accessories based on plant forms are painted with dye straight on to the fabric, emphasised with hand and machine stitching, appliqué and beads. Flowers and butterflies are stitched separately then applied to the articles so that they are almost detached from the fabrics on which they are sewn. The forms are based on drawings of plants and insects. *Crafts* magazine in July/August 1978 says that her work is 'a marvellous combination of richness and delicacy often reminiscent of English watercolour landscapes'.

Dorothy Reglar, after a post-diploma course at Birmingham College of Art and Design in 1966 worked for some time as an embroidery designer at Belville Sassoon. She then became a freelance fashion designer, also teaching part time in Hornsey College of Art. In the early seventies she was interested particularly in designing clothes for children. She is a versatile designer, using a variety of fabrics according to the type of article on which she is engaged. Her fine blouses incorporate old laces, her jackets have fine felt decorations. She also uses beads, sequins and embroidery, with smocking and quilting for garments. See figures 107, 108 and 109.

Pat Russell during the sixties and early seventies began to carry out more ecclesiastical embroidery, some of her designs based on lettering. She continues to design and work hangings and banners, screens and smaller articles for secular purposes, some evolved from her knowledge of heraldry and lettering, others based on stylised, almost geometric floral forms. Working for all denominations she has designed for four different alphabets: English, Greek, Bulgarian and Hebrew. She continues also with commissions for calligraphy, and has designed banners, maps and articles for interiors. As a relaxation she designs screens and hangings with ideas based on abstractions of flowers. (*Embroidery*, Volume 25, Number 4, Winter 1974.) See figures 9, 10, 11 and 168.

Barbara Siedlecka says that drawing is the basis of all her work. She has experimented with colour etching which has added depth and texture, developing into the use of fabric, paint, wax and plaster among other media. These have enriched the surface textures and also created atmosphere in her illustrations and embroideries. She draws from experience of her environment, the designs being formalised and abstracted, although remaining basically figurative. She says 'the more I learn, the more difficult this work becomes and the longer it takes'. See figures 98, 137 and 162.

Marion Stewart in the mid-seventies has worked on a larger scale, executing banners and hangings with geometric pattern, patchwork and padded areas. She is influenced by natural forms but the results are stylised and far removed from the original themes.

Gay Swift has specialised in machine embroidery, but is concerned with the dichotomy between pure drawing and the decadent, over opulence that embroidery offers. She finds the appropriate use of materials and the choice of colours in her work important. See figure 58.

Margaret Traherne has designed fabric structures for a number of public buildings, having become interested in large suspended and floating shapes strung across interior ceilings. These were in black and white or in brilliant colours, geometric in style. Later works include a set of banners flown at the Tate Gallery to commemorate the Gallery's seventy-fifth anniversary in 1977. She also designed a special group of banners in 1977 for the façade of Burlington House, hung for the Jubilee exhibition of the Royal Academy – British Art from 1953–1977. Her designs in the form of maquettes in fabrics were carried out to full scale in the workrooms of Tuttle and Pearce, flag makers.

Veronica Togneri keeps her weaving for particular purposes apart from her other work – appliqué, embroidery and patchwork. She enjoys working in traditional techniques and using natural materials but has no special bias, and produces domestic articles such as rag rugs, knitted and pieced blankets, using parts of old clothes and oddments of wools and other threads. She has been inspired by an eighteenth-century silk patchwork in the Victoria and Albert Museum based on the sub-divisions of a square into four, six and eight triangles arranged haphazardly and emphasised with embroidery. She tends to seek out groups of simple, geometric shapes that grow and break into new, interesting formations. (Some information from a 1976 Sunderland Arts Centre exhibition catalogue.) See figures 123 and 124.

Audrey Walker started to embroider during the mid-sixties, being concerned mainly with wall decorations, worked by hand. In 1972 she was commissioned to design and carry out a large panel for the Pump Room in Bath. She used both hand and machine techniques for this, completing the work in 1973. Her more recent embroidery combines both hand and machine techniques, dye and appliqué, to obtain a shimmering effect of merging colours. See figures 81, 82, 97 and 135.

Verina Warren started to work her small panels when she retired from Loughborough College of Art in 1972. In Derbyshire she was attracted by the countryside which was an inspiration as time went on. Her first show of work was with the Oxford Gallery in 1973 when she exhibited small, embroidered panels. See figure 149 and jacket.

Verina and Stewart Warren had a joint show in 1974 at 'New Faces' in the British Crafts Centre gallery. The work was small in scale, mainly in machine stitching with spray dyeing and painting, landscape the chief source of the work. Stewart Warren designed frames to suit the individual embroideries in order that a total effect could be achieved. This early work combined geometric with free pattern, some hand stitching, too. Gold thread outlines emphasised some shapes, the complete embroidery often being surrounded by a border of gold thread. The rigid geometric shapes contrasted with the naturalistic landscapes. Later a black period with almost black backgrounds and forms in a variety of textures, emerged for a short time, the inspiration for all the work being the Derbyshire landscape.

Kathleen Whyte continued to design and carry out commissions for churches as well as for other purposes. Her work is always strong in style, often with contrasting colours and textures, in which she is interested. She uses stitches to give both tone and colour and to express her ideas with economy of line and form. See figure 21 and colour plate 13.

Summary 1964–1977

Prominent people

Eugenie Alexander	Ione Dorrington	Zandra Rhodes
Dorothy Allsopp	Patricia Foulds	Christine Risley
Alison Barrell	Hannah Frew Patterson	Pat Russell
Judy Barry	Bill Gibb	Vera Sherman
Richard Box	Jennifer Gray	Eirian Short
Anne Butler	Sylvia Green	Lilla Speir
Joan Cleaver	Constance Howard	Margaret Traherne
Joy Clucas	Alison Liley	Audrey Walker
Joyce Conwy Evans	Moyra McNeill	Verina Warren
Barbara Dawson	Margaret Nicholson	Crissie White
Beryl Dean	Beryl Patten	Kathleen Whyte

Societies, schools, exhibitions, events

1964	Goldsmiths' School of Art selected as a centre for the Diploma in Art and Design
1965	Diploma in Art and Design also recognised at Birmingham, Loughborough, Manchester
1966	The opening of the Tay Bridge
1966	The Embroiderers' Guild Diamond Jubilee
1966	The *Hastings Tapestry*
1966	Contemporary Hangings in London
1967	Opening of the new Roman Catholic Cathedral, Liverpool
1968	The New Embroidery Group formed
1968	St Paul's Cathedral exhibition of ecclesiastical embroidery
1968	Presentation of the Hammersmith cope and mitre to the Cathedral
1968	Victoria and Albert Museum lectures by Joan Edwards
1969	The landing on the moon
1969	The *Overlord* embroidery started
1970	The Beckenham and Penge Textile studio inaugurated
1970	Gawthorpe Hall became a study centre for students
1971	The Crafts Advisory Committee formed
1972	Embroiderers' Guild Exhibition – Commonwealth Institute
1973	The Crafts Advisory Committee bought the Waterloo Gallery, London
1973	The British Crafts Centre retained Earlham Street
1973	The Practical Study Group was formed
1974	The *Overlord* embroidery completed
1974	A retrospective exhibition of Beryl Dean's work, including the embroideries for St George's Chapel, Windsor, and work of her students over the preceding 15 years
1975	The *Chester Tapestry* commenced
1975	A retrospective exhibition – 'Twenty-five years of embroidery' at the South London Art Gallery
1975	The Diploma in Art and Design became a BA Honours degree
1975	Trent Polytechnic recognised as a centre for the BA examination in textiles
1976	Embroiderers' Guild Exhibition, Commonwealth Institute
1977	The Queen's Silver Jubilee. The Silver Jubilee cope presented to St Paul's Cathedral

Main types of embroidery 1961 to 1969

Ecclesiastical embroidery, interest in metal thread work, *or nué*, gold kid
Use of found objects, stones, cardboard rings, shells, wood
Mid sixties a short period of 'sloppy' technique
Figurative design
Design for clothing decoration at the end of the sixties
Panels and hangings predominate in geometric and abstract styles
Mixed media increasing, use of dyes, screen printing
Soft sculpture using fabrics
Machine embroidery increasing in popularity

1970 to 1977

Interest in soft sculpture increases, padding and quilting
Food in fabric, as soft sculpture
Landscape dominates early seventies, although geometric styles popular
Mixed media-dyeing, screen printing, use of metal, wood, etc
Machine embroidery more popular than hand embroidery in colleges of art and polytechnics
Knitting increasing in popularity, used with embroidery as decoration
Patchwork developing during the late seventies

Books

1964	*The Art of Embroidery*, Marie Schuette, Sigrid Muller Christensen, Thames and Hudson
1964	*Samplers Yesterday and Today*, Averil Colby, Batsford
1964	*Embroidery, a Fresh Approach*, Alison Liley, Mills and Boon
1965	*Patchwork Quilts*, Averil Colby, Batsford
1965	*Blackwork*, Moyra McNeill and Elizabeth Geddes, Mills and Boon
1966	*Bead Embroidery*, Joan Edwards, Batsford
1966	*The Young Embroiderer*, Jan Beaney, Kaye
1966	*Inspiration for Embroidery*, Constance Howard, Batsford
1967	*Embroidery and Fabric Collage*, Eirian Short, Pitman
1967	*Creative Stitches*, Edith John, Batsford
1968	*Needlework Rugs*, Sybil Matthews, Mills and Boon
1968	*Simple Stitches*, Anne Butler, Batsford
1968	*Metal Thread Embroidery*, Barbara Dawson, Batsford
1968	*Ideas for Church Embroidery*, Beryl Dean, Batsford
1969	*Design for Embroidery*, Kathleen Whyte, Batsford
1969	*Canvas Embroidery*, Diana Springall, Batsford
1969	*Design in Canvas and Thread*, Aileen Murray, Studio Vista
1970	*Creative Appliqué*, Beryl Dean, Studio Vista
1970	*Canvas Embroidery for Beginners*, Sylvia Green, Studio Vista
1971	*Pulled Thread Embroidery*, Moyra McNeill, Mills and Boon
1971	*Lettering for Embroidery*, Pat Russell, Batsford
1972	*Canvas Work from the Start*, Anne Dyer and Valerie Duthoit Bell
1973	*Machine Embroidery: Technique and Design*, Jennifer Gray, Batsford
1973	*Machine Embroidery*, Christine Risley, Studio Vista
1974	*Quilting*, Eirian Short, Batsford
1974	*Canvas Work*, Jennifer Gray, Batsford
1975	*In Vogue*, Georgina Howell, Allen Lane
1975	*Creative Embroidery*, Anne Spence, Nelson
1976	*Machine Stitches*, Anne Butler, Batsford
1976	*Embroidery and Colour*, Constance Howard, Batsford
1976	*Needleworker's Dictionary*, Pamela Clabburn, Dover
1977	*Experimental Embroidery*, Edith John, Batsford

Magazines   *Embroidery, Crafts, Creative Needlecraft, Catalogues of Exhibitions*

**53 Right: 1970 – Sister Kathleen. A chasuble in lime green fabric with a
blue lining. The leaves are shaded from blue through brown-greens to bluish greens, with
the top ones in the reverse side of the lime green fabric. The trunk, branches and veins are
brown with outlines in antique gold thread. Made under the supervision of Beryl Dean**

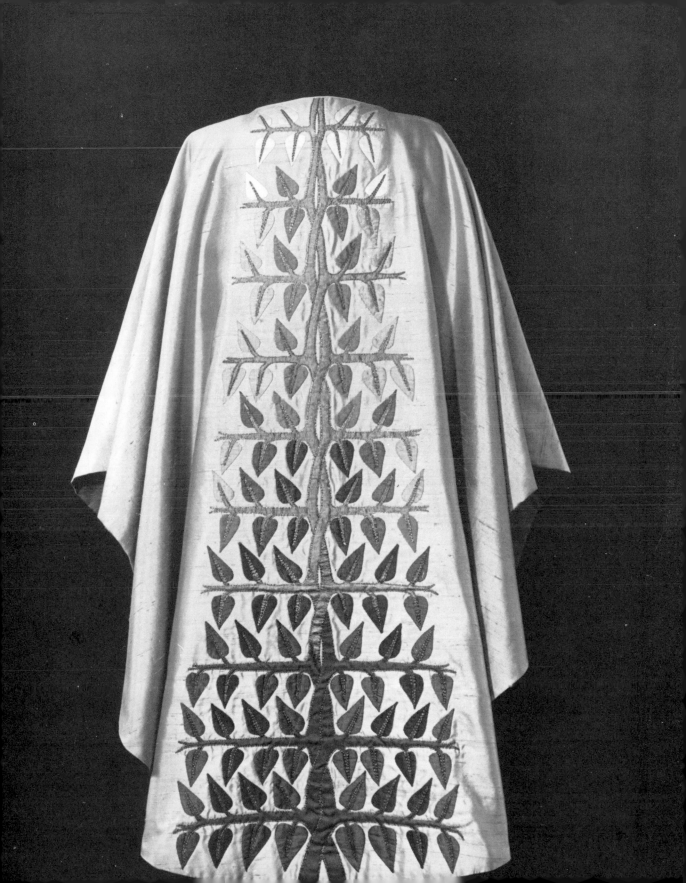

54 1970 – Michele Walker. *Diamonds.* **A quilt 75 in. × 90 in. (190.5 cm × 228.5 cm) in scarlet, black and white in pieced patches, with painted strips of small diamonds breaking the pattern horizontally**

55 1970 – Alison Barrell. *Chairman of the Board.* **Appliqué in felts and other fabrics. Machine and hand stitching with slightly padded areas**

56 1967-70 – Marjorie Morton and Elizabeth Carpenter. A festive cope for Eton. It depicts the Tree of Life, inspired by small photographs of Chinese paintings. The tree, growing from the rocks and the blue seas, emerges into smokey fire, billowing up the front of the cope. The Eye of God, or peacock's eye, is on the right of the tree. The background is in creamy gold Italian faille, with overlays in nets, silk and nylon organzas, metallic fabrics and threads. Couching is in gold, metallic and silk threads with some beads and sequins. *Photograph by Hills and Saunders*

57 1967-70 – Margaret Nicholson. Lady Banner. The subject is the Virgin and Child, richly embroidered with gold threads, gold kid, pearls and beads. On the reverse side the design shows a crown of thorns in gold kid with the words 'Coventry Cathedral'

58 1970 – Gay Swift. *Snow Queen.* **A detail of a panel in machine stitching. Freely worked in whites, greys, silver and blues, the fabrics pre-worked and applied, over padded card**

59 1970 – A scheme supervised by June Tiley for Bute Looms. Front view of a garment, using a variety of fabrics including suede. Appliqué with some padding, handwoven tweed, ribbon and patterned fabric

60 1971. A detail of garment

61 1970 – Joan Cleaver. Hand embroidery. Background a mauve even weave heavy furnishing fabric. Handsome shapes at left (which represent the scrap which is the foundation of the business) are in leathers moulded over each and built on top of each other and also straight stitches a sort of free herringbone! Circle was worked separately on canvas. 'I used knitting-wools and also made cords of mixed yarns to get a "glow" of colours.' Canvas 10.1 in. mesh. Here the ideas came from what is known as the 'drop out' of molten scrap in the furnaces. This circle was stretched on a sub frame and was slightly padded

62 Right: 1970 – Ruth Edmunds. Student at Birmingham Polytechnic. Saurer machine embroidered furnishing fabric using white thread on a black moygashal ground. A simple, small unit has been developed into a relatively large repeat. There is considerable interest in the tonal variation achieved by the change in direction of stitch. *Birmingham Polytechnic*

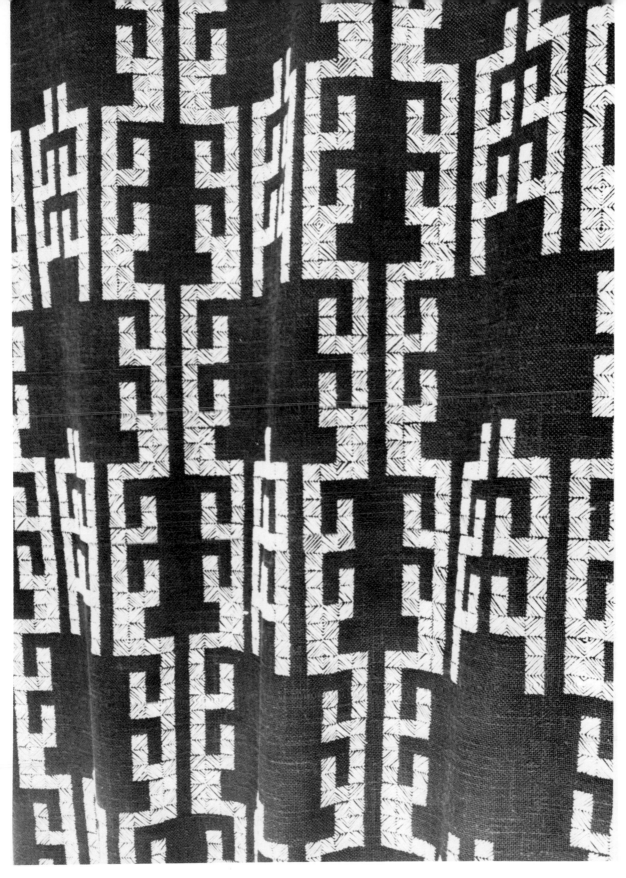

63 Left: 1970s – Annwen Nicholas.
Reverie Rouge. A panel 22½ in. × 16½ in.
(57 cm × 42 cm) worked on the Cornely
machine in mossing, with applied fabrics.
Owned by Mrs Sams

64 1970 – Lilla Speir. *Magic Garden.* An appliqué panel 31 in. × 38 in. (79 cm × 96.5 cm)
in plain and printed cottons and velvets, mainly blues and greens, on a vermilion
ground. The opened three-dimensional shutters disclose an eye in relief. *In the collection of
the Arts Council of Northern Ireland*

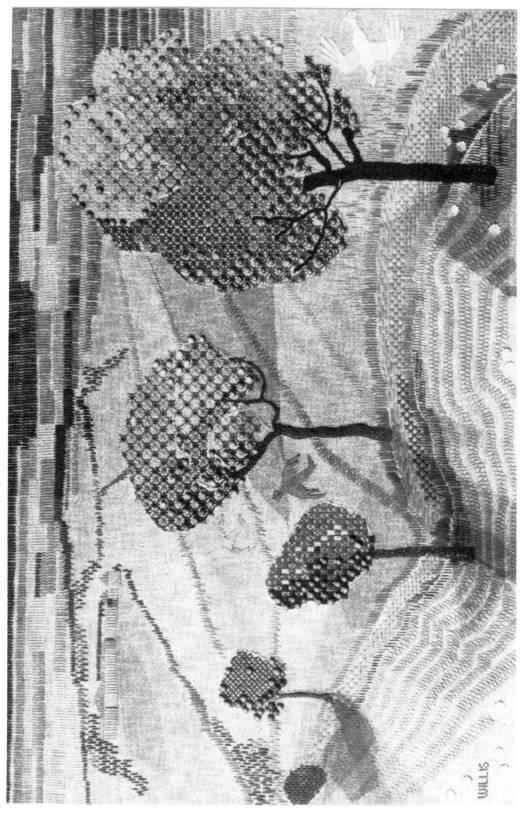

65 Left: 1970 – Rosamund Willis. *The Wolds from Friday Thorpe.* **A panel using a variety of stitches and fabrics.** *Loaned by Mrs J A Heslop*

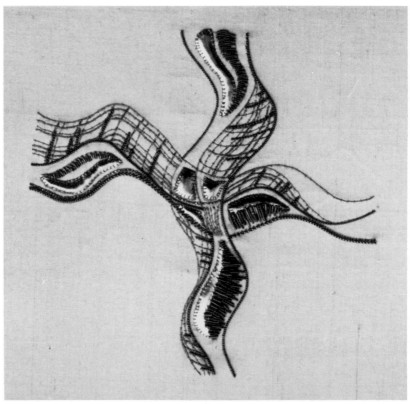

66 Right: 1970 – Joan Openshaw. A burse in gold threads and gold kid with silk stitchery

67 1971 – Bridget Pavitt. *Daisies in a Field,* **11½ in. × 14 in. (29 cm × 35.5 cm). Aged 11, Bridget Pavitt won first prize in the Junior Section of the summer competition organised by the Embroiderers' Guild. An ultramarine ground with white felt daisies, white perle cotton, stranded cotton and silver sequins, with green grass**

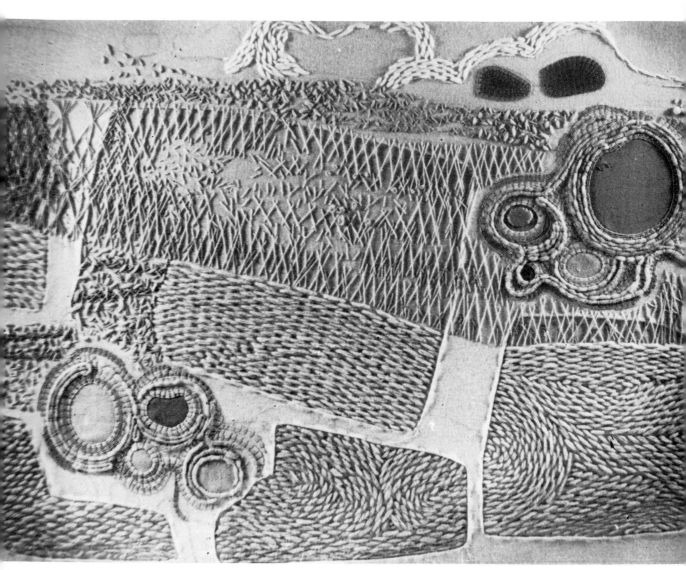

68 1971 – Janet Graham. A detail of landscape panel. *Shown at her exhibition in 1971*

69 1971 – Kay Macklam. Student at Goldsmiths' School of Art and the RCA. A panel 12 in. (30.5 cm) square, worked on calico in bullion knots in a variety of coloured wools, including greens, pink, purple and turquoise. The raised circles are in greys in stem stitch.
Photograph by Hawkley Studios

70 Far left: 1971 – Valerie Yorston.
Student at Goldsmiths' School of Art.
Cotton dresses hand painted in dyes on
yellow muslin with the figures of dolls
embroidered – front views on the front of
the dress, back views on the back

71 Left: 1971 – Becky Mullins. Student
at Goldsmiths' School of Art. A machine
knitted dress with hand embroidery

72 Right: 1971 – Diana Harrison. A machine quilted evening coat in white satin, screen
printed with a trellis design in grey, interspersed with clouds in a variety of colours
Left: Susan Rigg. A kimono of draped white organza screen printed with floating clouds
over navy and white cotton with applied flowers and stitchery in french knots. Both
students at Goldsmiths' School of Art

73 1971 – Pamela Rooke. A panel, 22½ in. × 23½ in. (57 cm × 60 cm), with applied pieces of bark, also lines of couched thread with a few interwoven threads

74 1970 – Alison Barrell. *Green Dorset*, 33 in. × 18½ in. (84 cm × 47 cm). A variety of fabrics is used including striped curtaining, tweed and velvet. Parts are padded. Colours are brown at the base, to blue-grey to green to turquoise, fawn, gold and ultramarine. *Embroiderers' Guild Collection*

75 1971 – Anne Butler. *League.* **A panel 7 ft × 9 ft (2.13 m × 2.74 m). It is in black and blue felt over card applied, also woven felt stripes and ribbons.** *Exhibited at the fifth Biennale in Switzerland. Owned by a Swiss museum*

76 Right: 1971 – Anne Butler. Detail of *League*

77 Early 1970s – Eirian Short. *Riding the Waves.* **A panel approximately 72 in. × 52 in. (183 cm × 132 cm) with the swan in white satin on shiny blue satin waves with painted lines**

78 Early 1970s – Eirian Short. *The Pearly Gates.* **The panel, approximately 60 in × 48 in.
(152.5 cm × 122 cm), is in high relief with white satin, padded clouds and a silver and
gold gate to heaven. The garden, worked finely, is in pinks, greens and other colours, with
beads, pearls and sequins. The work is mounted over board**

79 Early 1970s – Eirian Short. *In Loving Memory,* 48 in. × 36 in. (122 cm × 91 cm).
Various plain and patterned fabrics are mounted over board. Letters are stencilled

80 1972 – Heather Clarke. *Silver Supersheep*, **18 in. (46 cm) square. The sheep are crocheted in off white, the legs and heads in tent stitch in red. The field is blue shading to greens, in straight and canvas stitches, in appliqué of furnishing fabrics, felt and towelling. Straight stitches and canvas stitches, with a sky in silver metallic card, complete the work.** *Photograph loaned by the Embroiderers' Guild*

**81 1971 – Audrey Walker. *Out of Eden,
Morning and Evening.* A screen in three
panels, both back and front of each
embroidered. *Inside*: morning to evening
is represented with colours that have
been chosen to show the passing of time.
The left-hand panel has pale greens and
pinks as the theme while the centre panel
is slightly darker in tone and the right-
hand panel in considerably darker, and
sombre. This symbolises night and the
expulsion from the Garden of Eden.**

(Not illustrated)
***Outside*: the two narrower panels on this
side depict the figures of Adam and Eve,
one on each panel and almost filling the
frames. These figures are in applied
fabrics in a pale, pinkish brown colour
on green grounds and are simple
statements without the stylisation
associated with figure design. *Collection
of Dorothy Allsopp. Photograph by
Hawkley Studios***

82 1971-72 – Audrey Walker. *Pool in the Garden*, 8 ft × 4 ft (2.44 m × 1.22 m). Hand stitching, worked mainly in straight stitches with some cretan. In a variety of threads with shiny and dull textures

83 1972 – Diana Jones. *Undulating Patterns.* A canvas-work hanging with padding and wrapped tassels

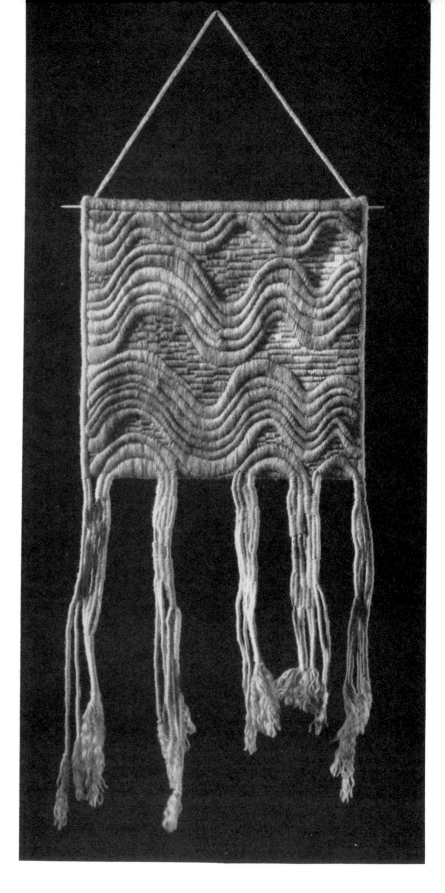

84 1972 – Jennifer Hex. *Red Wall*,
64 in. × 48 in. (163 cm × 122 cm).
Various materials on linen, with couched
threads and pleated and gathered areas
of fabric, also frayed edges in places and
different reds

**85 1972 – Beryl Greaves. Open
sandwiches in hand and machine
stitching. Slightly larger than life and in
a variety of fabrics, including organdie,
silk, cottons and skeins of thread**

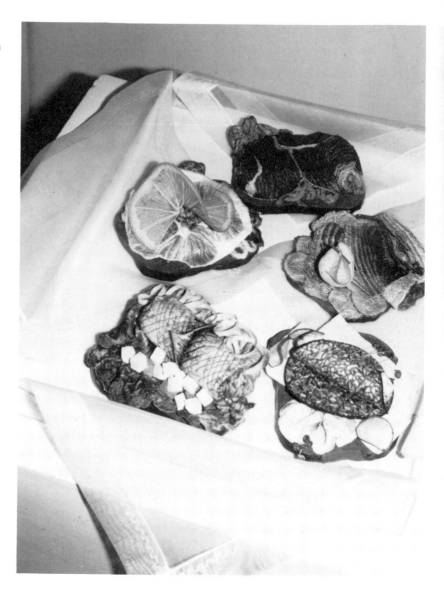

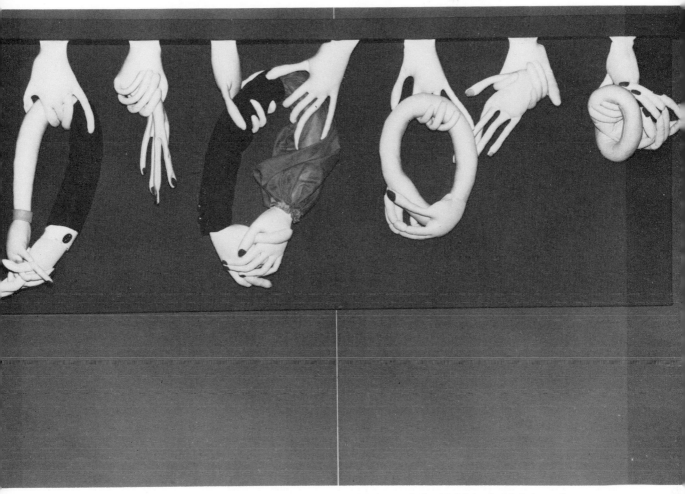

**86 1972 – Yvonne Dimmock. Student at Goldsmiths' School of Art. A panel
approximately 60 in. × 36 in. (152.5 cm × 91 cm). The background is red Welsh flannel,
the hands are three-dimensional life sized in cream fabric; two of the arms are in black
fabric**

87 1972 – Hebe Cox. *Brown Garden.* **A panel on cocoa-coloured denim, with appliqué in white, tan, dark brown and yellow. The embroidery is in couched black cord.** *Owned by Mrs Harding*

88 1972 – Heather Clarke. *Vase of Flowers*, 38½ in. × 22½ in. (98 cm × 57 cm). Flowers are in black and white, the curved shapes in a pinkish white satin. Over a pink ground black printed fabric is applied, with over this, part is covered with cellophane. *Exhibited with the '62 Group and the Embroiderers' Guild*

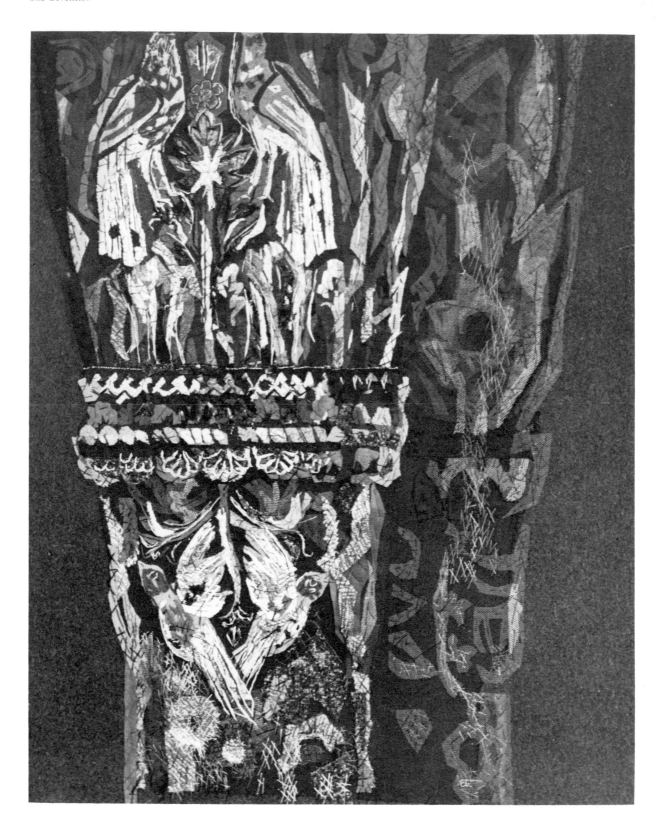

89 Left: 1972 – Esther Grainger.
Romanesque Capitals. A panel 30 in. ×
24 in. (76 cm × 61 cm). An embroidery
and collage using woollen fabrics and
nets, stitched in stranded cottons.
Collection of The Rev John Rutherford.
Photograph by Ramsey and Muspratt Ltd

90 1973 – Esther Grainger. *ICI
Reposent,* a panel. *Collection of the
Welsh Arts Council*

91 1973 – June Tiley. A panel in canvas-work 20 in. × 15 in. (51 cm × 38 cm) in green, turquoise, white, dull pinkish mauve, pink and red threads

92 1973 – Averil Colby. Patchwork 22 in. × 25 in. (56 cm × 63.5 cm) made for Valerie Dickens (née Winter) for her baby, Claire. Cotton dress and furnishing fabrics and prints. The main colour is blue, with floral prints in mixed colours on a white ground. The border is dark blue cotton. *Photograph by J S Newton-Claire*

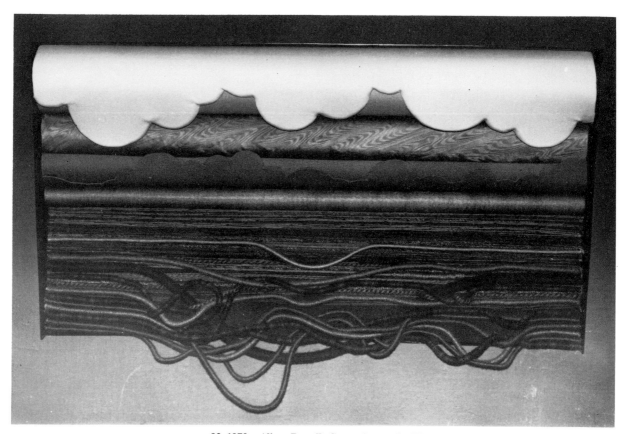

93 1973 – Alison Barrell. *Storm Across the Water.* **The theme is taken from an Elton John song. Tubes (paper and carpet) covered in various fabrics, form storm clouds rolling in over the seascape. Straight stitch, knitted tubing and covered tubing of varying thickness represent tangled waves**

94 Right: 1973 – Barbara Millie. Student at Goldsmiths' School of Art. A full-sized room construction with life-sized figures, stuffed and bandaged. The idea is based on the astronaughts and the moon landing. The pattern background is painted; plastic, unbleached calico, white stretch fabric, bandage and other fabrics are employed. Some hand stitchery emphasises parts of the composition. *Photograph by John Hunnex*

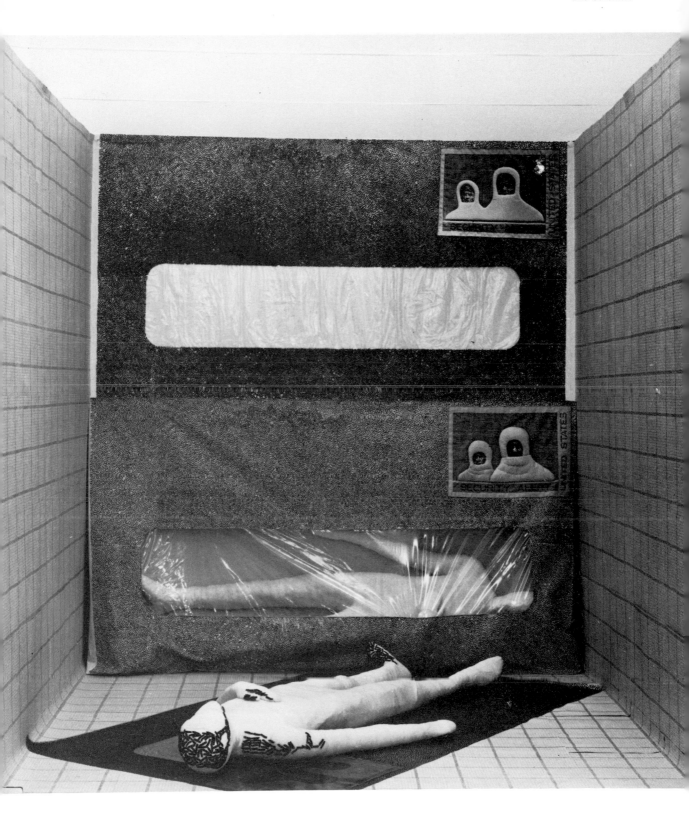

95 Right: Early 1970s – Malcolm Lockhead. Designs for St Mungo's Shrine, Glasgow Cathedral. Cloth arranged as patchwork with a grid in overlays in gold and silver. Kneelers in two different designs, have grid-like patterns, symbolic of the cranes on the River Clyde. The work has been carried out by the Glasgow and the West of Scotland Branch of the Embroiderers' Guild. Shown here is a detail of the patchwork and grid

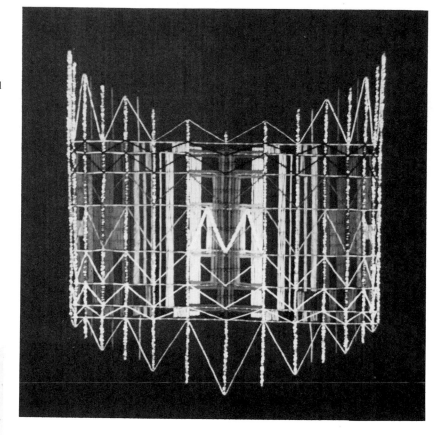

96 Left: 1973 – Yvonne Dimmock. Student at Goldsmiths' School of Art. A dress based on Gothic architecture, the sleeves decorated with appliqué. Embroidered in red, green, black and white, with black and white stripes

97 Right: 1972-73 – Audrey Walker. *Monarchy 1000.* A panel 9½ ft × 7½ ft (2.90 m × 2.29 m) hung in the Pump Room at Bath. This panel was in commemoration of the crowning of Edgar, the first king of all England, in Bath Abbey in AD 973. Nine vertical panels suggest the nine royal houses. At the top of each panel the reigning monarch is applied in gold kid, while at the bottom a list of the reigning monarchs of each house is in gold kid lettering. In the centre 'the struggle for power' is shown, from the Viking invasion to the bombing of St Paul's in the Second World War. The colours blend with the Pump Room and are mainly blues, greens, grey, turquoise and cream. This photograph shows a detail in process of being worked

98 Left: 1973 – The Beckenham Textile Studio. *House and Garden*, 9 ft × 5 ft 6 in. (2.74 m × 1.68 m). A commission given to the Studio by the Embroiderers' Guild. Designed by Barbara Siedlecka and shown at the *Daily Mail* Ideal Home Exhibition 1973, as an entrance to the Embroiderers' Guild stand. A number of students worked the panel, so it was divided into sections and as four weeks only were allowed for this, the bulk of the embroidery was carried out at home. The background is lavender felt, the house white with blue-grey clouds in stretch nylon jersey over foam and card. The bushes and flowers are entirely made of pompons in dark green, orange, pink and red wool. The grass is wool, in Ghiordes knots in various greens, while the earth is in browns in free canvas stitching. The paving is grey fabric over card with couched threads. The trees are knitted and crocheted

99 1973-74 – Herta Puls. *Illusion*, 23½ in. × 33½ in. (60 cm × 85 cm). The centre is designed from drawings of perspective in layers of poplin. Light blue, light and dark brown and olive green are the main colours. The frame is in sections covered in cotton, velvet, leather and organdie. In the San Blas technique of cutting fabrics from the top layer to reveal those underneath

100 1973 – Lorna Tressider. *Postcards are Forever,* **11½ in. × 13½ in. (29 cm × 34 cm). Appliqué with machine embroidery**

101 Right: 1974 – Lorna Tressider. A panel in machine stitching, *Enclosed Fantasy* **in applied fabrics in a variety of textures**

102 Left: 1974 – Anne Butler. A hanging 24 ft × 9 ft 7.32 m × 2.74 m) in a Methodist church, Timperley, Manchester, worked in three pieces in appliqué, in red, yellow, green and blue on navy blue. *Photograph, Garth Dawson and Company*

103 1974 – Judy Barry and Beryl Patten. Altar curtains and altar panels for the main altar of St Andrew's Church, Droylsden, Manchester. The curtains are 13 ft high × 20 ft wide (3.96 m × 6.09 m)

On the Continent richer materials were liked to work on, and designs were more flamboyant and richly embroidered. A detail at Selba Chenault, buttons could be made of precious metal and set with jewels.

During the 18th Century Bath was one of the centres of fashion where these people wearing richly embroidered clothes could be seen taking the waters at the Pump Room, & at the Assembly Rooms. The Costume Museum there contains many valuable examples of these garments, including waistcoats.

Salisbury Museum also has a good collection of these waistcoats in various materials, colours and styles. Also a number richly embroidered in silk, and in gold and silver work.

This waistcoat chosen for study had been in the collection since 1942. It had been dated circa 1774 which must have been about the time it was embroidered and made up.

It was made for the 12th Earl of Shelly and had been well worn but the colour of the embroidery had faded very little.

Waistcoat made an interesting study because of the great variety of materials and embroidery designs used.

104 Left: 1974 – Mary Greening. A sheet of researched work prepared for the City and Guilds examination. Mary Greening was a student at Chippenham Technical College, history of embroidery being a part of the course. *Photograph by Hawkley Studios*

105 1974-75 – Elizabeth Hammond. The Canterbury hanging, 36 in. × 60 in. (91 cm × 152.5 cm). A communal undertaking designed by Elizabeth Hammond and worked by members of the East Kent Branch of the Embroiderers' Guild. One working party carried out individual parts of the embroidery while another party assembled the hanging. A key to the items on the banner is worked on the reverse side. Fabrics include linen, gold and silver kid and nets for search lights. The hanging is in the Senate Building of the University of Kent in Canterbury

**106 1974 – Mavis Lee. A textural
sampler 36 in. × 24 in. (91 cm × 61 cm)
by a part-time student in Anna
Wilson's adult education class. It is
worked in off-white and beige threads;
stitches include sheaf filling, button hole,
wrapped stitches, long chain and
needleweaving**

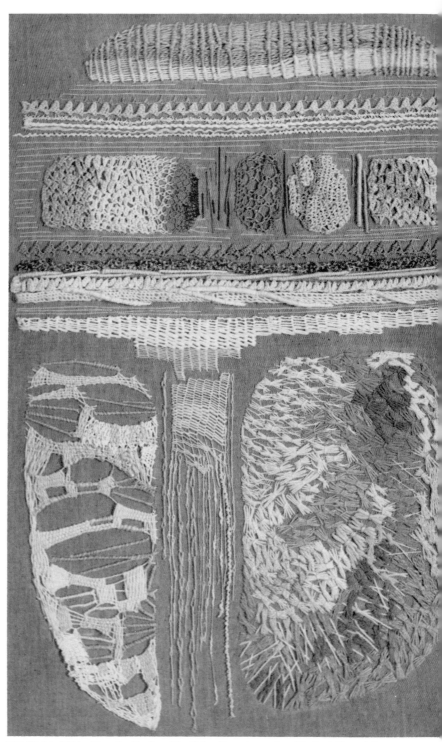

107 Right: 1974 – Dorothy Reglar. *The Fairy Tree.* **A panel on black cloth, mainly
worked in white and silver in straight stitches, fly stitch, beads and sequins.** *Exhibited in
the '62 Group exhibition 'Embroiderers at Work'*

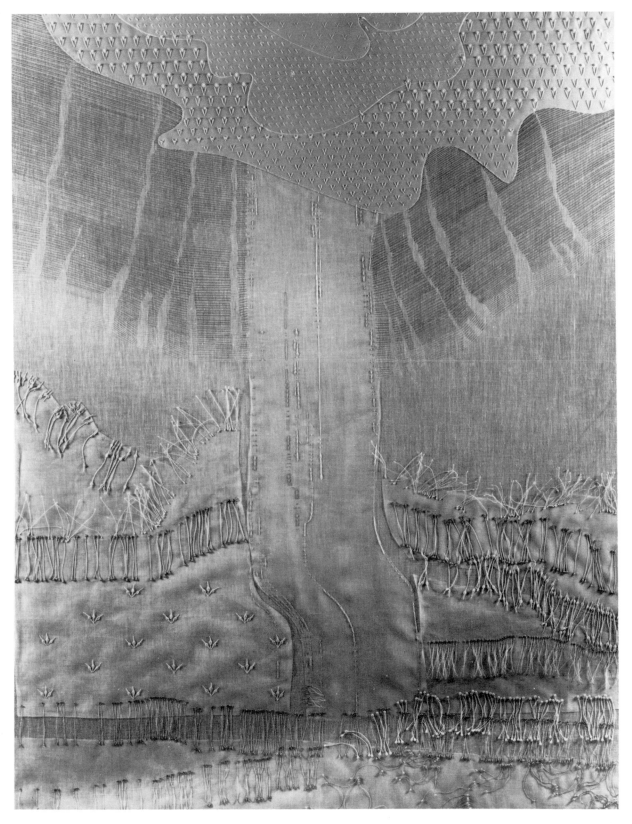

108 1969 – Dorothy Reglar. A black chiffon dress, decorated with metal shapes, sequins and beads

**109 1974 – Dorothy Reglar. A detail
of a smock, with appliqué and stitchery**

**These two garments show a diversity
of style and approach to design**

110 Left: 1974 – Sally Crowle. Student at Goldsmiths' School of Art. A panel approximately 16 in. × 20 in. (40.5 cm × 51 cm). The background is canvas with a painted wardrobe and garments worked in satin stitch in brilliant colours and white

111 1974 – Beryl Chapman. *Dark Centre*, a panel. Screen printing with embroidery

112 1974 – Isabel Clover. Festival cope on cream furnishing fabric, depicting the four winged creatures of the Gospels. Appliqué in gold and lime Thai silks with brown curtain sheer, shot gold/black fabric and brown/black tweed. Embroidered in french knots, stem, cretan and padded satin stitches, in wool and silk threads, with padded kid and trade beads. *Exhibited at St Alban's in 1980. Loaned by permission of St Mary's Church, Dedham, Essex. Photograph by Mrs S Hilderth-Brown*

113 1974 – Isabel Clover. A detail of the festival cope

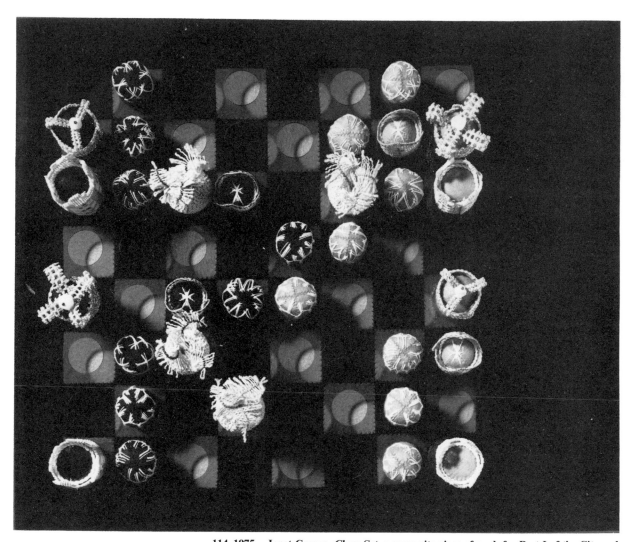

114 1975 – Janet Craggs. *Chess Set,* **a composite piece of work for Part I of the City and Guilds examination. The chess set is designed to hang on a wall. The idea behind this is that by moving the chess pieces the complete pattern may be changed. The perspex box has holes drilled in the top layer to hold the chess pieces. The base is in patchwork in black and red felt, with a black felt border. Various techniques and stitches are used, including counted-thread work and metal thread embroidery**

115 1975 – Jennifer Hex. *Flower Patch***, 19 in. × 21 in. (48 cm × 53 cm). Various threads, mainly in reds and greens with small areas of orange, purple and others. Worked in satin stitch on linen**

116 1975 – Elspeth Crawford. *Magic Square*, **4 ft (122 cm) square. The background is purple hessian, the inner square in mustard-coloured hessian, with a red crushed velvet centre. Embellishment is with gold and velvet braids and ribbons and coloured beads. The embroidery is by hand**

117 1975 – Anna Wilson. *African Mask*. An experimental embroidery 24 in. × 18 in. (61 cm × 46 cm) in the nature of a sampler

118 1975 – Jennifer Shonk. Student at Loughborough College of Art and Design. *A Wedding Breakfast.* **Three dimensional composition using screen printing, dyeing, hand and machine embroidery**

119 1972-75 – Lilian Dring. *Parable II* – 'In the (polluted) heavens above . . .' A collage made entirely from waste materials; refuse, plastics, fabrics, meat bones, garden rubbish, sweet papers, plastic flowers, inner tubes of ballpoint pens, broken toys, newspaper, telex tape, etc. (*Parable I* on a wartime theme is illustrated in *Twentieth-Century Embroidery to 1939*)

120 Mid 1970s – Sheila Ashby. *Oops.* **A panel with needlelace.** *Photograph by Gail della Pelle*

121 Right: 1970s – Sheila Ashby. *Elan.* **A panel 30 in. × 40 in. (76 cm × 102 cm). Needlepoint lace mounted on fabric.** *Photograph by Gail Della Pelle*

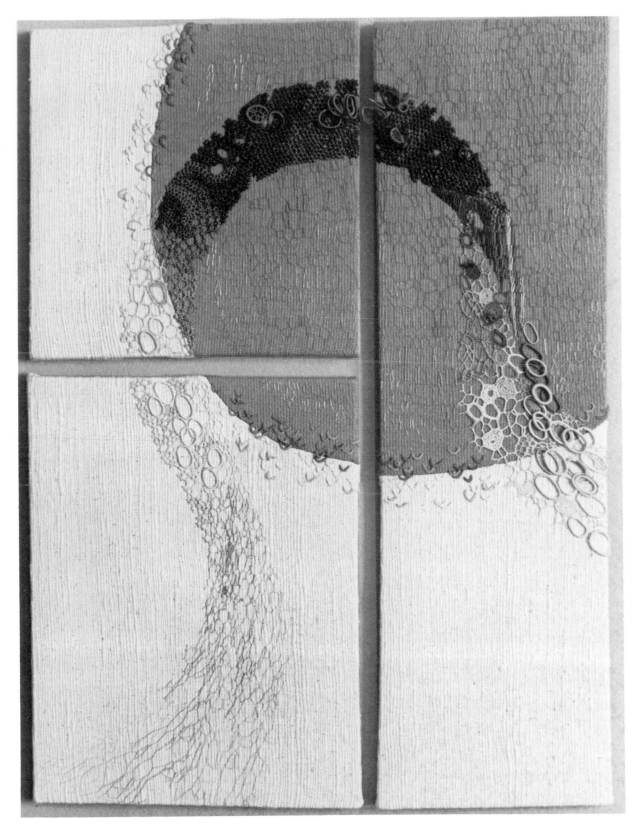

**122 1975 – Rosamund Willis. *Aysgarth
Falls*. A panel using various stitches.
*Owned by Colonel Hall***

123 1976 – Veronica Togneri. *The Unthrift Sun*, 80 in. (203 cm) square. Cotton patchwork. Colours mainly blues and oranges with some patterned fabric

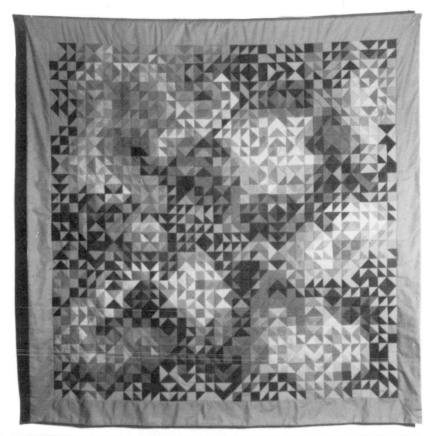

124 Below: 1976 – Veronica Togneri. Detail of *The Unthrift Sun*

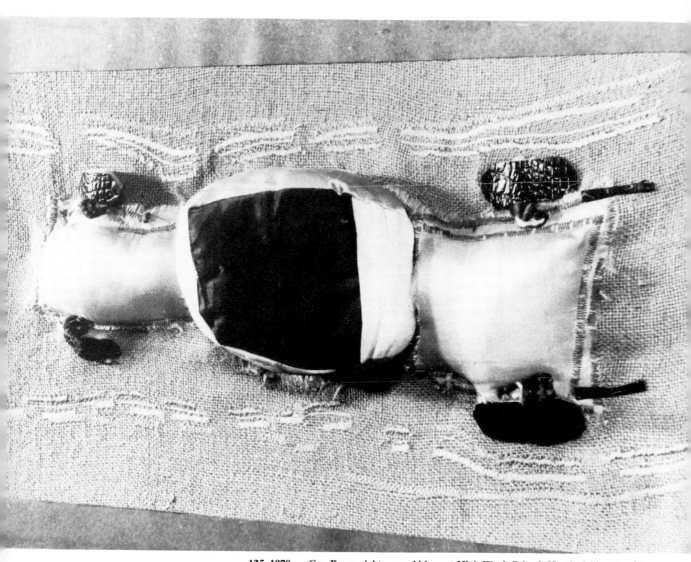

125 1970s – *Car*. By an eight-year old boy at High Wych School, Hertfordshire, taught by Jane Page. Padding, satin and leather are used with hand and machine stitching

126 1970s – *Harp.* By a nine-year old
girl at High Wych School,
Hertfordshire, taught by Jane Page.
Hand and machine stitching are used

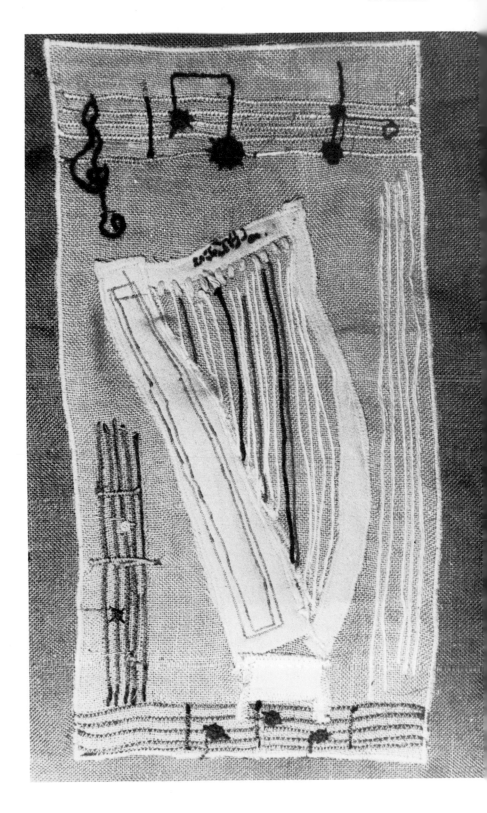

127 1975 – Alison Barrell. *Winter Hill.* **An off white landscape. The round forms at the top and base are in papier mâché made over a child's toy. The papier mâché is cut to make the fields which are padded and covered with fabrics of velvet, corduroy, cotton, linen and muslin. The shapes are sewn together to make the original sphere. Covered buttons and polystyrene balls make the trees**

128 1976 – Eileen Phipps. Student at Doncaster School of Art. Caliban for *The Tempest.* An example of costume embroidery for City and Guilds examination

129 Below: 1976 – Maureen Helsdon. *Enigma Variations*, 45 in. × 24 in. (114 cm × 61 cm). Screen printed lettering, photo litho photographs printed on fabric, all cut up and reassembled. Appliqué of cotton, silk and linen with machine stitching

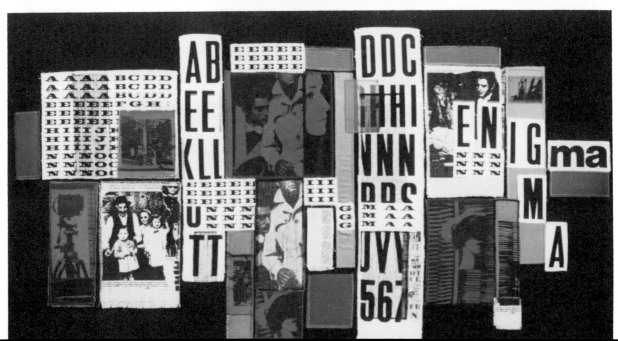

130 1975 – Mary Ward. *Optics 7*,
36 in. × 48 in. (91 cm × 122 cm). A
panel in yellows, browns, pinkish greys,
tan and ochre in blanket stitch on a
black ground

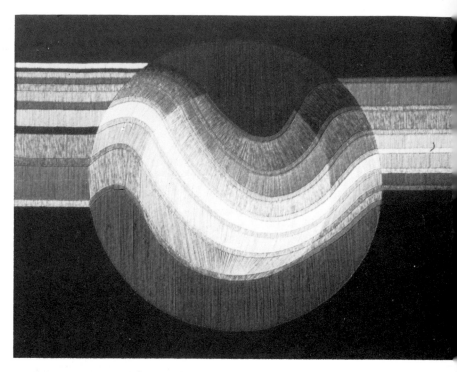

131 1976 – Mary Ward. *Optics 9*,
36 in. × 48 in. (91 cm × 122 cm). A
panel in blanket stitch; pale blues, pinks
to reds, pale mauves to purples, yellow,
greenish yellow are stitched on a black
ground

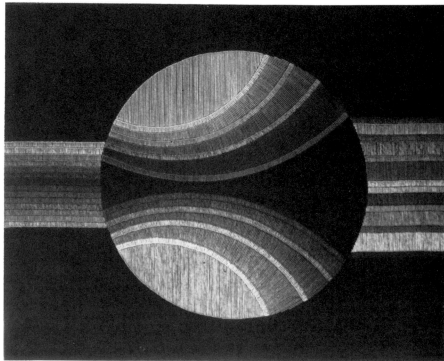

**132 Mid 1970s – Crissie White.
Canvas-work panel in silk and wool. The
idea grew from the fact that each person
is different but all are inextricably linked
and dependent on one another, of
varying significance but of equal value**

**133 & 134 1976 – Audrey Tucker. Two
small panels.** *Day into Dark*, **each
approximately 3½ in. × 4½ in. (9 cm ×
11.5 cm). Worked from drawings of an
apple tree seen during different parts of
a day for seven days in order to note
colour and tone changes during the
morning through to the evening. Her
findings were that in duller light the tree
had more colour than during the lighter
part of the day, when the tones, too,
appeared lighter.** *Owned by Dorothy
Allsopp. Photograph by Hawkley
Studios*

135 1976 – Audrey Walker.
Thunderstorm, 36 in. (91 cm) square, in
a variety of threads in white, greys,
grey-blues and very dark greys. French
knots and straight stitches, bullion knots
and loops are used for the embroidery

136 Right: 1976 – Vicki Ames. Student at Goldsmiths' School of Art. *Red and Green Faded Rug*, 39 in. × 25½ in. × 34½ in. × 27½ in. (100 cm × 65 cm × 88 cm × 70 cm).
Machine embroidery using the Tufting machine, the Bernina tacking foot and the Cornely machine for moss stitch, with satin stitch on the Irish machine. Colours are in faded pink to dull red, with greyish greens

137 1976 – Barbara Siedlecka. Textile mural in Hounslow Civic Centre, 10 ft × 17 ft (3.05 m × 5.18 m). Designed by Barbara Siedlecka and worked with the help of Alison Barrell, Marjorie Self, Nancy Kimmins and Margaret Gaby of the Beckenham Textile Studio. The mural is in the Members' Dining Room, it is stitched in wools on canvas, with carpet applied to give pile textures. The design is based on a general view of the river and features in the environment. The colour is cool in contrast to the red brick walls of the room, in greys, blues, and greenish greys, with darker colour at the base to lighter at the top. Large textured areas at the top and bottom of the hanging are non-pictorial, non-abstract

138 1976 – *The Kingdom, the Power and the Glory*, 6 ft (1.83 m) high. Commissioned by Canon Peter Spink, then of Coventry Cathedral, for the chapel of a community centre. Wool on canvas in a variety of stitches and textures. The shape had to fit an existing alcove. In red, blues and yellow, with various shades of brown

139 Left: 1970s – Daisy Lambert. A panel in appliqué 15½ in. × 10¼ in. (39 cm × 26 cm). Flowers in yellow, orange, pinks, blue, with a patterned fabric vase in green, yellow, orange and blue and leaves in bright green; all on a turquoise cotton ground. *Photograph by Hawkley Studios*

140 1976 – Dorothea Nield. *Golden Bouquet.* **Framed as an octagon, 17¾ in. (45 cm) across. An experiment to maintain a good technique, using inexpensive gold threads, plastic beads, sequins and net. Worked on a dull gold furnishing fabric**

141 Left: 1976 — Elspeth Crawford. *Abbey Triptych.* **A detail of a panel 30 in. × 34 in. (76 cm × 86.5 cm) in heavy lace, felt, cotton and net on a silver cloth background. Worked in machine embroidery**

142 1976 – Elspeth Crawford. A vase of flowers, part of the *Abbey Triptych* **panel. In lace, felt, cotton and machine embroidered**

143 1976 – June Tiley. *Celtic.* **A
patchwork quilt, 4 ft 6 in. × 6 ft 6 in.
(1.37 m × 1.98 m), in plain and
patterned fabrics, commissioned by the
Crafts Council of Wales for the
National Eisteddfod. In the
January/February 1977** *Crafts* **magazine
the quilt was described as 'beautifully
subdued'**

**144 Far right: 1976 – Lindy Siew Keow
Oon, a student from Malaysia and
studying at the London College of
Fashion. Two versions of one design
using beading and machine embroidery:
(1) Faces with fringe in purple and blue,
using acetate, chenille, bugles and beads;
(2) The same design in cording with wool
fringe, used in conjunction with
knitwear**

145 Left: 1976 – Margaret Hall. *Girl in a Garden,* 10 in. × 9½ in.
(25.5 cm × 24 cm) complete. Mainly in hand embroidery,
except for the pot and the border which are in machine
stitching. Stitching is in couched machine thread on a yellow/
red shot silk background. Some seeding, detached buttonhole
and french knots are also worked in the machine thread. The
girl was drawn from life and sits in a spacially flat symbolic
garden, towered over by a huge urn which has men's heads on
the handles

146 1976 – Margaret Hall. Detail of *Girl in a Garden*

47 1976 – Sylvia Green. A red frontal for St Michael's Church, Highgate, London. Commissioned by Mr and Mrs J Gosling, designed by Sylvia Green and made by her and members of the St Michael's Embroidery Group. In gold, white wool and purple silk, applied to red dupion. Worked in jap gold threads and wine, gold, red and purple silk threads. The symbols are in shapes and colours to represent the attributes of sainthood rather than a specific saint. The purple and white represent the dark and light sides of human nature, while gold represents the transformation of human nature by the Holy Spirit.
Photograph by John Gay

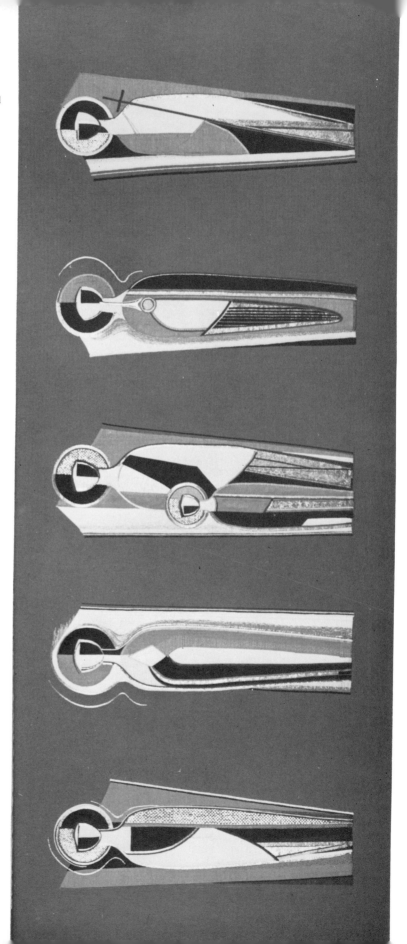

148 1976 – Sylvia Green. A detail of the frontal. *Photograph by John Gay*

149 1976 – Verina Warren, *Aureola* **(halo of light), approximately 15 in. (52 cm) square. A landscape of trees is surrounded by another circle of trees and an outer circle. Hand and machine embroidery and dye; in greens, golds, blue and grey**

150 Right: 1976-77 – Hannah Frew Paterson. A sheet of ideas for a pulpit fall 20 in. × 13 in. (51 cm × 33 cm), from which the 23rd Psalm pulpit fall for the Gorbals Parish Church was carried out. *Embroiderers' Guild Collection.* **See also colour plate 10**

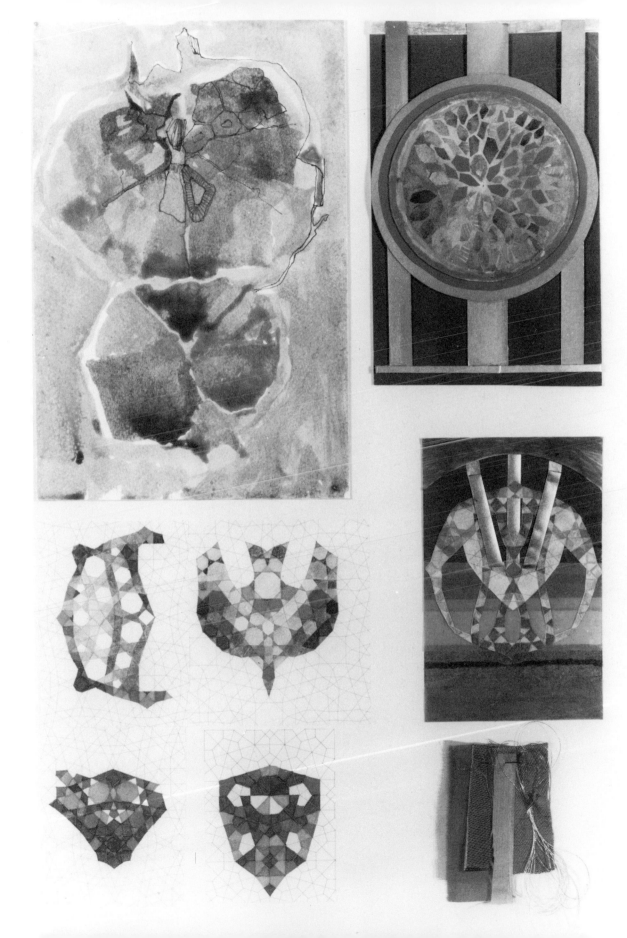

151 1970s – Nancy Kimmins. *Lot's Wife,*
**36 in. (91 cm) high. Worked on rug
canvas with tufting graduating from six-
ply rug wool at the base to two-ply
crewel wool at the apex. Skeined loops
at the base with cut and uncut pile**

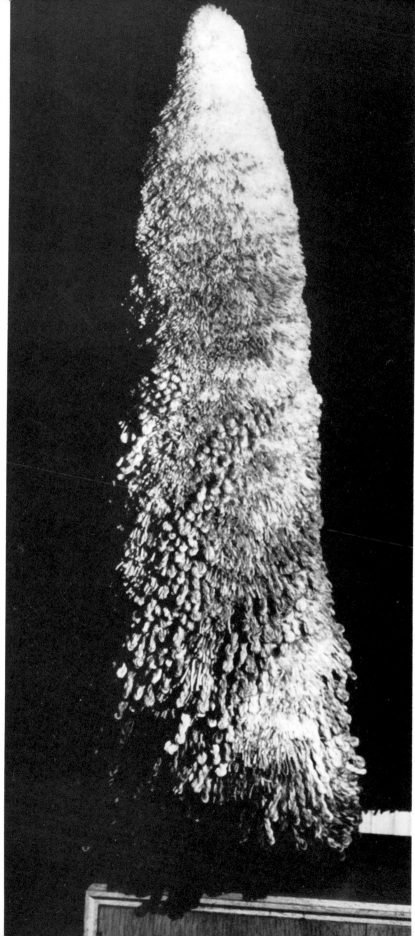

152 Mid-1970s – Diana Jones. *Mille Fiore,* **24 in. (61 cm) square. Based on an Italian glass paperweight. In shades of blue and natural colours, with some yellow, brown, red and green**

153 1970s – Joan Nicholson. Examples of 'multiples' for canvas embroidery by courtesy of Messrs J & P Coats Ltd. The patterns may be interchanged and put together to make new ones and the worker can add or subtract patterns as required

154 1977 – Barbara Dawson. *Ray of Sunshine.* **Embroidery on canvas, 10 in. × 8 in.
(25.5 cm × 20 cm).** *Owned by the Department of the Environment*

155 Mid 1970s – Stanley W Lock. A bead sample in black and white beads, the design inspired by wine glasses. The black beads are in shiny glass, the white ones china and duller. Worked on transparent nylon. *Photograph by Hawkley Studios*

156 1977 – Karen Spurgin. *Shaggy Square*. Rags, wood and threads hand stitching

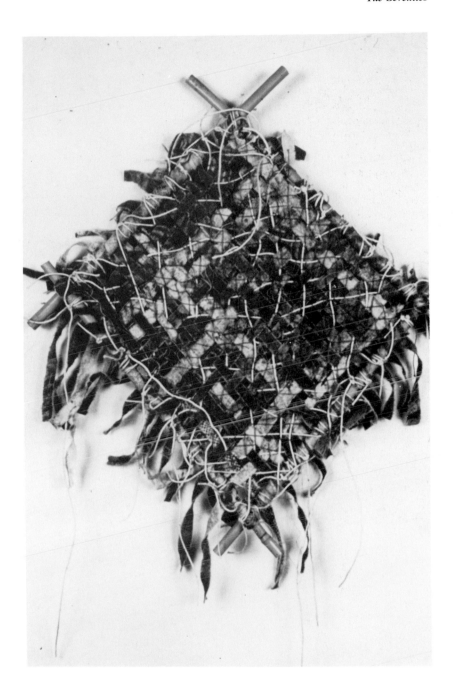

157 1977 – Beryl Dean. A gold mitre for the Bishop of Lewes, Sussex

158 Far right: 1977 – Beryl Dean. Pulpit fall for the ancient church of East Guildeford, near Rye, Sussex. In brilliant reds, purples and blues, embroidered on cloth of gold.
Photograph by Millar and Harris Ltd

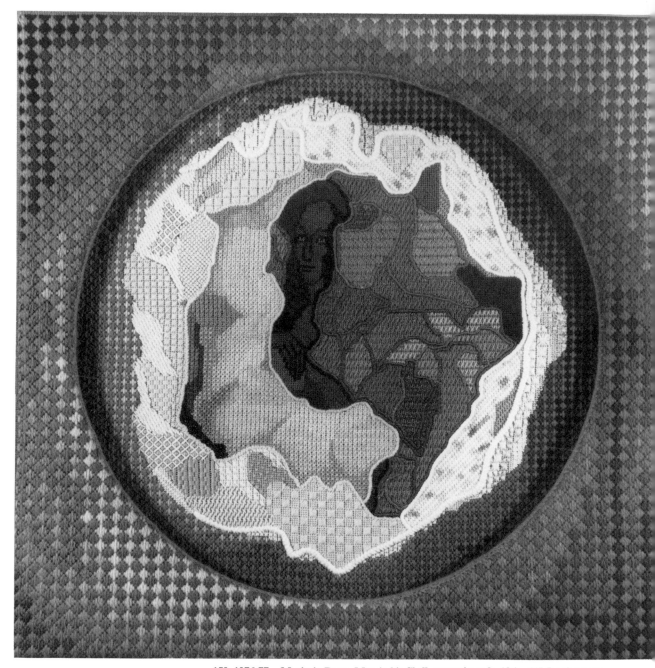

159 1976-77 – Marjorie Dyer. *Man in his Shell,* approximately 18 in. (45.5 cm) square. The idea is to express people shying away from the world and other people, isolated and missing the glory expressed by the fiery colours of reds, purples and oranges that surround the shell. A variety of other colours is used. The work is entirely on canvas in wool and silky threads, with overlaid cording

160 1977 – Lilla Speir *Heavenly Pastures.* **A quilt 7 ft 4 in. (2.24 m) square. An idyllic Galloway landscape in appliqué and patchwork with a padded central panel in relief. Mainly blue, green and white cotton.** *Owned by Mrs Stenhouse*

161 1977 – Elaine Waller. *Feast*, approximately 7¾ in. × 8 in. (19.5 cm × 20 cm).
Darning on coarse scrim in a variety of threads and colours. The border is black and
brown. Sequins and beads in different colours are introduced too

162 1977 – Barbara Siedlecka. *Living City,* **9 ft 6 in. × 7 ft 6 in. (290 cm × 229 cm).
Designed from a series of sketches made in Europe. Worked in wools on rug canvas with
areas of applied carpet.** *Owned by Credit Suisse, London*

163 1977 – Polly Hope. *Red Coat, 58 in. (147 cm) in length. A variety of fabrics is used. Exhibited in a show of 'Stuffed Pictures' at the University Art Gallery of New York and Albany. Photograph by Patrick Matthews*

164 Polly Hope. Another view of the red coat, which was exhibited in New York and in 1980 at the National Theatre. *Photograph by Hawkley Studios*

165 1976-77 – Elizabeth Hammond. A
purple hanging, 4 ft × 10 ft 6 in. (1.22 m
× 3.20 m), for Advent and Lent in St
Peter the Delce, Rochester, Kent.
Designed by Elizabeth Hammond and
worked by ladies of the Parish, part time
at the Medway College of Design,
Rochester. Fabrics include velvet, felt,
pvc, kid, with textures in knitting,
crochet, macramé and metallic threads

166 1977 – Judy Barry and Beryl Patten. A stole, one of several for a scheme for Manchester Cathedral High Altar furnishings. Machine embroidery, the design using the dove theme

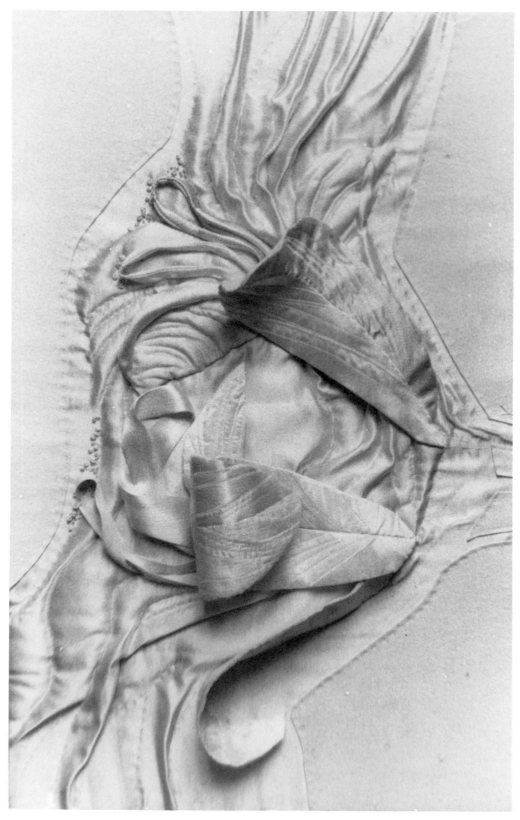

167 Left: 1977 – Kirsty McFarlane. *White Lilies*, 20 in. × 30 in. (51 cm × 76 cm). Ivory satin is folded, pleated and padded, with additions of stiffened, machine embroidered silk panels and rouleaux of silk and satin with surface stitching in white and ivory. Flat areas are masked in ivory felt. The complete work is framed in a clear perspex box

168 1977 – Pat Russell. A set of red copes for Norwich Cathedral. The chevron patterns are machine quilted; also a frontal in cream, gold and vermilion fabrics, for the High Altar

169 1977-78 – Crissie White. *Joseph's Coat of Many Colours.* Technicolour dream coat in patchwork in various fabrics. *A commission for Dundee Royal Infirmary*

170 1977-78 – Margaret Wingham. A sample on a canvas background, worked in various stitches. Tree trunks are in violet suede. Violet, steel blue, dirty purple and brown leathers are also used. *Photograph by Hawkley Studios*

171 1975-77 – Beryl Dean. The Silver Jubilee Cope. The idea was conceived in 1975 and based on the steeples and towers of churches within the See of London. A golden effect with an overall delicacy was to be achieved. The background of the cope is in cream wool, with silk organza appliqué in delicate colours. A variety of synthetic metal threads is used for the embroidery, carried out by a number of embroiderers in Beryl Dean's class at the Stanhope Institute, therefore the towers and steeples have been worked separately and applied to the ground later.
Photograph by Millar and Harris Ltd

172 1977 – Constance Howard. *Jubilee.*
A hanging, 7 ft × 4 ft (2.13 m × 1.22 m),
looking into a window seen during
Jubilee celebrations. A variety of fabrics
and threads is used, the window covered
in couched threads of wool in varigated
colours from blue to white and pink to
white. Machine and hand stitching.
Northampton Museums and Art Gallery.
Photograph by Beedle and Cooper

Bibliography

COLBY, Averil, *Quilting*, Batsford, 1972

JONES, Mary Eirwen, *A History of Western Embroidery*, Studio Vista, 1969

EDWARDS, Joan, *Bead Embroidery*, Batsford, 1966

HALLS, Zillah, *Coronation Costume, 1085–1953*, Her Majesty's Stationery Office, 1973

HOWELL, Georgina, *In Vogue*, Condé Nast, 1975

HUGHES, Therle, *English Domestic Needlework*, Lutterworth Press, 1966

LAVER, James, *The Liberty Story*, Liberty & Co. 1959, reprinted 1971

MACCARTHY, Fiona, *All Things Bright and Beautiful, 1830 to today*, Allen & Unwin, 1972

PEVSNER, Nikolaus, *Pioneers of Modern Design*, Pelican, 1960

RISLEY, Christine, *Machine Embroidery*, Studio Vista, 1973

THOMAS, Mary, *Dictionary of Embroidery Stitches*, Hodder and Stoughton, 1934

THOMAS, Mary, *Embroidery Book*, Hodder and Stoughton, 1936

Magazines, Catalogues, Periodicals and Booklets

Crafts from 1964

Embroidery from 1964

The Hastings Embroidery booklet 1966

Catalogue of Embroiderers given by the Needlework Development Scheme 1965

Index

Page numbers in *italics* refer to illustrations.
Those following names of individuals/organizations refer to
illustrations of their work